LEARN LACECRAFT

Audrey Vincente Dean

A Sterling/Main Street Book
Sterling Publishing Co., Inc.   New York

To Cheryl of satins and lace,
who says it's her turn now

The author thanks the following companies which helped with materials for this book: Berisfords for velvet and satin ribbons; J & P Coats for threads; Dylon for multi-purpose and cold-water dyes; John Lewis Partnership, Oxford Street, London, for lace trimmings; C.M. Offray & Son Ltd for ribbon; E.W. Roper & Son Ltd, Nottingham, for lace trimmings and for a lace-covered lampshade; Silvan Ltd, London, for lace trimmings.

Thanks also to Westphal Creative Collection, Germany for two collage designs; Hungerford Arcade, Hungerford, Berkshire, for lace curtain and bedspread; Victoria's Bedroom, Hungerford, Berkshire, for brass bedhead.

Designed and edited by TL Creative Services
Series Editor Eve Harlow
Photography by Di Lewis
Illustrated by Terry Evans and Tracey Davis

10 9 8 7 6 5

A Sterling / Main Street Book

Published in 1990 by Sterling Publishing Company, Inc.
387 Park Avenue South, New York, N.Y. 10016
Originally published by William Collins Sons & Co Ltd
© 1987 by Audrey Vincente Dean
Distributed in Canada by Sterling Publishing
% Canadian Manda Group, P.O. Box 920, Station U
Toronto, Ontario, Canada M8Z 5P9
Printed in Hong Kong
All rights reserved

Sterling ISBN 0-8069-7344-7

Contents

Introduction

1 Lace in the Home

2 Lace and Needlework

3 Lace and Crafts

4 Sewing with Lace

Introduction

The word 'lace' means romance and luxury to most people, and its charm has been acknowledged through the ages. For hundreds of years, lace was coveted and much of it has been preserved in the nature of family heirlooms. Today, thanks to the abundance and variety of machine-made lace, it can be applied lavishly to clothing, furnishings and accessories.

This book is about the many crafts associated with lace. Fine sewing, embroidery, appliqué are familiar techniques; new applications for lace are also to be found — beading, machine embroidery, jewellery-making, lace collage, dyeing and flower-making.

All the techniques of using lace are included, so that everything you make will have that exquisite, hand-worked look. You will have the pleasure of creating something of elegance and charm for yourself or a valued gift for your friends.

Getting to know laces, to recognise the different types and their uses, is part of the fascination of lacecraft. A Lace Collection is provided overleaf to help you to develop your expertise in this fascinating craft.

Double wide lace insertion

Lace collection

All the modern, machine-made laces and broderie types used throughout the book are shown here. Most commercial lace is made of nylon. Some pure cotton, cotton and other fibre mixes, and polyester laces are also available. Choose cotton, cotton-mixtures or polyester laces if the item being trimmed is likely to need frequent laundering.

Cotton lace edging

Cluny lace

Macramé lace

Guipure edging

Lace insertion

Galloon lace

Guipure motifs

Leavers lace edging

Gathered Leavers lace

All-over lace

Lace insertion beading

Galloon beading lace

Broderie beading

Broderie edging

Gathered broderie edging

Chantilly lace

Lace in the Home

Lace used for trimming home furnishings adds elegance and charm to almost any decorative scheme. In this chapter, bed linen, table linen, lampshades and cushions are trimmed with luxurious lace. The glamorous cushions pictured here are made of washable fabrics and lace and in spite of their fragile appearance, they are eminently practical.

Luxury cushions

If you love the prettiness of lace and ribbons and treasure exquisite furnishings these cushions could be your first lacecraft project. Sewing with lace is not difficult but there are certain important techniques to learn, which help to produce the delicate, hand-sewn effect.

Heart cushion

Materials required
Finished size (without ruffle)
38 × 37cm (15 × 14½in)
45cm (½yd) of 120cm (48in)-wide polyester satin fabric
20cm (8in) of 120cm (48in)-wide Chantilly lace fabric with scalloped edges
2m (2¼yd) of 10cm (4in)-wide lace edging
1.20m (1⅜yd) of 18mm (¾in)-wide lace beading
2.50m (2¾yd) of 9mm (⅜in)-wide double face satin ribbon
Squared pattern paper, 1sq=5cm (2in)
Heart-shaped cushion pad

Preparation
Draw the pattern (Fig 1) up to full size on squared pattern paper. Cut out the paper pattern. From the satin fabric cut two pieces 45cm (18in) square.

Pin the paper pattern to the wrong side of one satin piece (cushion front) and work basting stitches round the pattern. Unpin the paper pattern and re-pin to the wrong side of the second satin piece (cushion back). Pencil round the outline, then cut out 12mm (½in) from the pencilled line.

From the Chantilly lace cut the motifs from both ends of the strip including the scalloped edges, leaving 12–25mm (½–1in) net all round the motifs. Cut other motifs from the lace in the same way.

Join the short ends of the lace edging and gather up the straight edge, leaving the gathering stitches in (see Lacecraft Techniques 1, page 8).

Working the design
Pin the scallop-edged motifs to the right side of the cushion front, positioning them in the upper curves of the heart shape. Arrange and baste other motifs on the heart shape (see picture).

Sew the motifs to the cushion front either by hand, working whip stitches all round the outline of the lace motifs (see Lacecraft Techniques 1, page 8), or by machine, straight-stitching just inside the edges of the

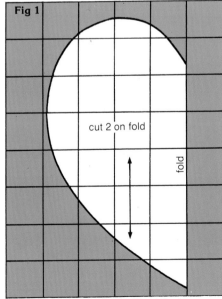

Fig 1 *Graph pattern for the Heart Cushion, 1sq=5cm (2in). Draw and cut out from doubled pattern paper*

Fig 1

cut 2 on fold

fold

motifs. Cut away the excess background net after stitching, close to the motif edges.

Finishing

Cut out the heart shape, cutting 12mm (½in) from the pencilled line. Make up the cushion cover (see below).

Pull up the gathering thread on the prepared lace edging to fit around the cushion. Hand-sew to the cushion cover and then hand-sew the lace beading over the ruffle's edge, stitching along both edges of the beading.

Thread ribbon through the beading, tying the ends in a bow at the top of the cushion.

Bolster cushion

Bolsters are the easiest cushions to make — the luxury look comes from using pretty fabric and a lot of lace!

Materials required

Finished size (without ruffles) 15cm (6in) diameter and 40cm (16in) long
50cm (20in) of 120cm (48in)-wide polyester satin fabric
3.75m (4⅛yd) of 10cm (4in)-wide lace edging
1m (1⅛yd) of 2.5cm (1in)-wide lace beading
3.50m (3¾yd) of 6mm (¼in)-wide double face satin ribbon
4 guipure flower motifs
2 lace butterfly motifs
Bolster cushion pad

Preparation

Cut a piece of satin fabric 50×60cm (20×24in). Measure to find the centre and pin the four flower motifs in a group with the butterflies at each end of the group (see picture).

Working the design

Apply the lace motifs by hand or by machine as for the Heart Cushion. Join the long edges of the fabric with machine-stitching and press the seam open. Turn a double, narrow hem on both short ends to make casings for ribbon.

Cut the lace edging into four equal pieces and join the ends of each piece. Gather along the long edge (see Lacecraft Techniques 1). Baste and then zigzag-stitch a ruffle at each end of the tube of fabric, so that the

ruffles are about 38cm (15in) apart. Baste and stitch the second ruffle in the same way, about 2.5cm (1in) nearer to the tube ends.

Cut the ribbon into four equal pieces. Cut the beading into two pieces. Thread a piece of ribbon through each piece of beading, then baste and stitch the beading round both ends of the bolster, over the inner ruffles. Tie the ribbon ends in bows.

Finishing

Thread ribbons through the casings at the bolster ends. Slip the bolster cover on to the pad and draw up the ribbons, tying the ends in bows.

Square cushion

Materials required

Finished size (without ruffle) 30cm (12in) square
40cm (16in) of 120cm (48in)-wide cream polyester crepe de chine

LACECRAFT TECHNIQUES 1

Joining lace end to end

Lengths of flat lace are joined by overlapping the ends and oversewing the edges. Match the pattern if possible for an almost invisible join. If lace is more than 2.5cm (1in) wide, turn the cut ends under before overlapping and sewing. Very wide laces, of 6–15cm (2½–6in), are best joined by cutting out round the pattern motif on both ends, and overlapping and stitching as for joining all-over lace (see Lacecraft Techniques 3, page 26).
Note: No. 50 machine embroidery cotton thread is recommended for all sewing with lace.

Gathering lace edging

Pretty pre-gathered laces are widely available but they have a rather heavy heading, which can spoil the delicate effect when applied to lingerie or children's clothes. Lace edging, gathered by one of the methods described here, looks far prettier and is very simple to apply.
Gathering by hand Most hand-made and some machine-made lace edgings have a heavy thread running along the straight edge. Find this thread with a

Making cushion covers

The quickest — and easiest — way to make a square, rectangular or round cushion cover is to make it without a fastening.

Pin and baste together the two pieces of fabric of the same size for the front and back of the cushion cover, right sides facing. Stitch 12mm (½in) from the edges and leave a gap in the seam of about 25cm (10in).

Turn the cover to the right side through the gap. Press the seams and then, after the cushion pad has been inserted through the gap, hold the open seam edges together and oversew to close.

If a frill or ruffle is to be applied round the edges of the cushion, work as follows. Join the ends of the frill or ruffle, then pin and baste it round the edges of one piece of the cushion cover, on the right side. Match the straight edges of the frill or ruffle to the edges of the cushion cover. Stitch to the fabric. Lay the second piece of cushion cover on top, right side down. Baste together, then stitch round again on the same line of stitches and leaving a gap in the seam for turning the cover and inserting the cushion pad. Finish the seam with oversewing from the right side.

22cm (8½in) square cream polyester
satin fabric
2 white organdie motifs
1m (1⅛yd) of 2.5cm (1in)-wide white
lace beading
1.50m (1⅝yd) of 6cm (2¼in)-wide
cream lace edging
2m (2¼yd) of 10cm (4in)-wide white
lace edging
2.50m (2¾yd) of 9mm (⅜in)-wide
cream double face satin ribbon
Square cushion pad

Preparation

Cut two 33cm (13in) squares of crepe
de chine. Baste the square of satin to
the centre of one piece on the right
side.

Working the design

Baste the organdie motifs to the
satin square (see picture for
arrangement). Apply the motifs by
hand or by machine as for the Heart
Cushion.

Join the ends of the cream lace

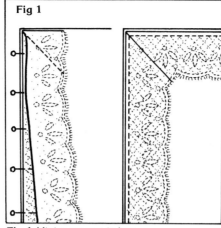

Fig 1 *Mitring corners in lace*

edging and gather the long edge to
fit around the satin square (see
Lacecraft Techniques 1). Stitch with
zigzag stitches.

Thread ribbon through the
beading and cut off excess. Cut the
ends of the lace beading diagonally.
Hand-sew the beading around the

satin square, starting at a corner and
folding the cut end under, and
stitching over the edge of the cream
lace ruffle. Gather the beading a little
as you sew and mitre the corners
neatly (Fig 1). Finish the last corner
by folding the cut edge under to
simulate a mitred corner.

Cut the remaining satin ribbon
into four equal pieces. Tie a bow in
the middle of each piece and sew the
bows to the corners of the beading.

Finishing

Join the ends of the white lace
edging. Gather it up to fit around the
cushion front and baste in position,
right sides and straight edges
together.

Lay the cushion back on top, right
sides facing, and make up the
cushion cover (see opposite page).

---

needle-point and use it to pull up
gathers. For a full ruffle, allow two and a
half to three times the finished length.
Gathering by machine If the lace has
no heavy thread, set the machine for a
long stitch and loosen the top tension
a little. Work two rows of stitching
along the straight edge of wide lace
edgings, and a single row of stitching
for narrower, 12–25mm (½–1in),
edgings. Pull up the gathers.

Applying gathered lace to fabric

If the gathered lace is being applied to
fabric as a surface ruffle (for instance,
on the outline of a yoke), baste the
lace in position and work a very fine
zigzag stitch along the edge of the
lace. Alternatively, straight stitching
can be used but it is more likely to be
visible.

To apply a gathered lace ruffle to
the raw edge of fabric (such as for a
fabric frill), work as follows:
1. Pin and baste the gathered lace
along the edge of the fabric, right
sides facing, with the lace heading
about 6mm (¼in) from the fabric
edge.
2. Set a zigzag stitch wide enough to
catch the lace heading and go right off
the edge of the fabric. The stitch will
catch the raw fabric edge into the lace
as you sew. Work the stitching slowly
and stop every 5cm (2in) or so to

adjust the gathers you are about to sew.
3. Turn the work to the right side and
press along the seam. Work a very
narrow zigzag stitch along the seam
from the right side (Fig 1).

Making galloon ruffles

Galloon makes a very pretty ruffle as
it has two decorative edges. It is a
particularly effective trim for items
that have a hemmed or finished edge
(Fig 2).
1. Machine-gather the galloon lace
about 9mm (⅜in) from one edge.
2. Pull up the gathers and stitch to the
fabric with a straight stitch, working
over the machine-gathering line.

Whip stitching

Whip stitching is a useful technique
for finishing the cut edges of lace or
tulle and can also be used for hand-
applying lace motifs to fabric or net.

Use No. 50 machine embroidery
cotton thread or a pure silk thread,
matching the colour closely.

Whip stitching is worked from right
to left.
1. Do not tie a knot in the thread end.
Instead, lay about 2.5cm (1in) of thread
along the edge you are whipping and
catch the end in as you sew.
2. As you near the end of the thread,
cut off the end to about 2.5cm (1in)
and lay the new thread alongside the
old, whipping over both (Fig 3).

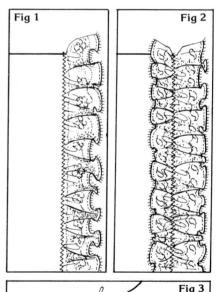

Fig 1

Fig 2

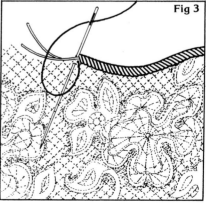

Fig 3

Light and lacy

Lace makes the prettiest lampshades. While the fabric does not have sufficient bias stretch for making shaped shades, it is ideal for such shades as the Tiffany shape in the picture. An all-over cotton lace with a floral motif has been mounted over pink silk, with a deep ruffle added at the bottom edge and a narrow ruffle at the top. Velvet ribbon trim adds the finishing touch. By using lace over fabric, it is possible to mask the fact that the fabric underneath may not precisely match other furnishings.

Estimating fabric quantities

To estimate fabric for a lampshade frame of a different size from the one pictured, measure the frame from top to bottom ring and add 2.5cm (1in) to the measurement. Measure round the frame at its widest point and add 2.5cm (1in). This gives you the amount of lace and lining fabric you will need for your lampshade.

Measure round the bottom ring and double the measurement for the amount of wide lace edging needed for the ruffle. Measure round the top ring and double it for the amount of narrow lace edging needed for the ruffle at the top.

Tiffany lampshade

Materials required

Finished size 25cm (10in) deep (without ruffle) and 97cm (38in) round widest part

- 30cm *(12in)* of 120cm *(48in)*-wide pink silk (or similar) fabric for lining
- 30cm *(12in)* of 120cm *(48in)*-wide all-over cotton lace
- 1m *(1⅛yd)* thin, round elastic
- 2.15m *(2⅜yd)* of 7.5cm *(3in)*-wide lace edging
- 60cm *(24in)* of 4cm *(1½in)*-wide lace edging
- 1.10m *(1¼yd)* of 6mm *(¼in)*-wide pink velvet ribbon
- 1 skein white lampshade binding tape
- Tiffany lampshade frame to dimensions of frame pictured or as desired
- Latex adhesive

Preparation

If the frame is an old one you are reusing, check for rust spots. The frame must be rubbed clean with fine sandpaper and re-painted with a quick-drying gloss paint.

New frames will already be white-painted. Bind the top and bottom rings of the frame with binding tape, finishing ends with a few stitches.

From the lining fabric cut a piece 28×99cm *(11×39in)*. Cut a piece from the all-over lace to the same size.

Working the design

Join the short ends of the lining, right sides facing, taking a 12mm *(½in)* seam. Trim the seam allowance and neaten the edges with oversewing. Turn a narrow hem on one edge and then gather the hem, leaving the gathering threads hanging.

Make a 6mm *(¼in)* casing on the other edge to take the elastic. Leave a gap in the casing and then insert the elastic. Knot the ends loosely.

Slip the lining on the frame, right side of fabric to the struts. Pull up the gathering stitches so that the top edge of the lining fits the circumference of the top ring. Pin, then oversew the lining to the top ring. Finish off the gathering threads with backstitches.

Smooth the lining over the frame, then gently pull up the elastic so that the bottom edge of the lining just turns under the bottom ring. Knot the elastic ends together, then close the gap in the casing with hemming.

Join the short ends of the all-over lace, right sides facing, taking a 12mm *(½in)* seam. Trim the seam. Slip the lace cover on to the lining, right side out. Pin the bottom edge to the bottom ring, right on the edge. Oversew the lace to the bottom ring, taking stitches through to the taped ring. Gather the top edge to fit the top ring. (If the lace stands above the ring, trim it neatly.)

Now oversew the lace to the top ring, taking stitches through to the taped ring. Remove the pins.

Putting on ruffles

Join the ends of the wide lace edging and gather the straight edge to fit the bottom ring (see Lacecraft

Techniques 1, page 8). Using small running stitches, sew the ruffle round the lampshade.

Work the top ruffle in the same way, using the narrow lace edging.

Finishing

Cut a piece of the velvet ribbon to fit round the lampshade just above the bottom ruffle. The ends should just touch. Glue the ribbon round the lampshade, using tiny spots of adhesive. With the remaining ribbon a small bow can made made and sewn over the join.

Ideas for lacy lampshades

Drum-shaped lampshades are the easiest to cover. Try the effect of ribbon and lace bands for a pretty bedroom shade. Bind the top and bottom rings with lampshade tape. Cut pieces of 4cm (1½in)-wide satin ribbon the depth of the shade plus 12mm (½in). Cut strips of 4cm (1½in)-wide lace insertion to the same measurement. Glue or stitch the lace and ribbon to the top and bottom rings, stretching the strips taut. Trim off any excess lace and ribbon. Finish top and bottom rings with pieces of 12mm (½in)-wide velvet or satin ribbon, glueing them in place (Fig 1).

For a romantic look, cover a lampshade with spotted net mounted over a plain fabric and sew cut-out motifs of guipure or all-over lace to the lampshade (Fig 2).

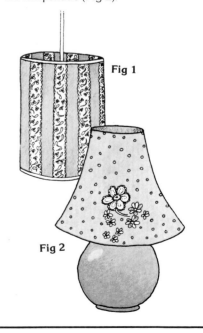

Fig 1

Fig 2

Romantic bed linen

The bed linen in the picture is made of washable, moiré-patterned polycotton sheeting and is trimmed with cotton Nottingham lace.

The quantities of lace used in making the bed linen is given but if you decide on a different arrangement it is advisable to work out the design on paper first.

Lace is inclined to pull up a little in stitching so always estimate a little extra – about 10cm (4in) on the width of a sheet. This allowance has been made in the quantities of lace given below.

Sheets

Materials required

For one plain sheet and one lace-trimmed sheet
Finished sheet size (without lace trim) 275cm (108in) long by 230cm (90in) wide
5.70m (6¼yd) of 230cm (90in)-wide sheeting
2.40m (2⅝yd) of each of the following laces: 7cm (2¾in)-wide Vandyke-style lace edging (A); 3cm (1¼in)-wide lace insertion (B); 4cm (1½in)-wide lace insertion (C)

Preparation

Cut the sheeting into two pieces across the width, to make two sheets 285cm (112in) long. Join laces A and B edge to edge (see Lacecraft Techniques 2, page 16).

Working the design

Bottom sheet Turn a 6mm (¼in) hem, then a 3cm (1¼in) hem to the wrong side on one end and machine-stitch.

Turn a 6mm (¼in) hem, then a 6cm (2¼in) hem to the wrong side on the other end and machine-stitch.

Top sheet Make the same hems on the top sheet as on the bottom sheet. The lace is applied to the end with the 3cm (1¼in) hem.

Neaten one end of the joined strip of laces A and B. Pin and baste along the hem on the right side of the sheet so that the lower edge of lace B is aligned with the stitching line of the hem. Work a short zigzag stitch along the same stitching line and be prepared to ease the basting stitches if the lace is taken up in stitching and begins to pucker.

Cut off any excess lace at the edge of the sheet, then machine-stitch across the short ends of lace B to make a neat finish.

Lace C is worked next. Insert this into the sheet 2cm (¾in) away from the straight edge of lace B (see Lacecraft Techniques 2, page 16).

Finishing

On the sheet pictured, twin-needle machine-stitching has been worked either side of inserted lace C, with a row of fancy machine embroidery stitching above. A second row of the same fancy stitch has been worked just above lace B.

When a little colour is required to match a furnishing scheme, work the embroidery in coloured threads.

Pillowcases

Materials required

For two pillowcases
Finished size (without lace ruffle) 50 × 75cm (20 × 30in)
1.20m (1⅜yd) of 230cm (90in)-wide sheeting
7.30m (8yd) of each of the following laces for edging ruffle: 7cm (2¾in)-wide Vandyke-style lace edging (A); 3cm (1¼in)-wide lace insertion (B)
3m (3¼yd) of 3cm (1¼in)-wide lace insertion (B) for diamond shape
2.15m (2⅜yd) of 4cm (1½in)-wide lace insertion (C) for bands

Preparation

From the sheeting cut four pieces 53 × 78cm (21 × 31in). Cut two pieces 53 × 15cm (21 × 6in) for pillowcases inside flaps.

Cut each of laces A and B into two equal lengths. Join laces A and B edge to edge (see Lacecraft Techniques 2, page 16) to make two ruffle lengths of 3.65m (4yd).

Working the design

Work the diamond-shaped insertion on two of the pillowcase pieces before making up (see Fig 1 below and Lacecraft Techniques 2, page 16). Mitre the corners neatly (see page 9 for technique).

Cut lace C into four pieces each 53cm (21in) long. Insert a strip of lace across the width of the pillowcase pieces at each end, just touching the points of the inserted lace diamond shape (Fig 1).

To complete the effect, a row of

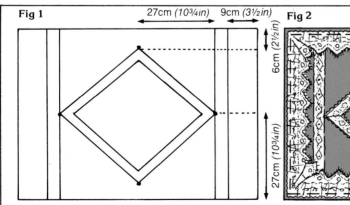

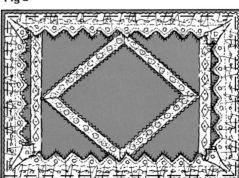

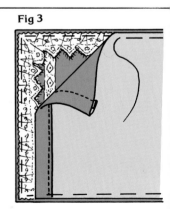

Fig 1 *The pillowcase front, showing the position of lace insertion*

Fig 2 *Baste the ruffle all round pillowcase front*

Fig 3 *Lay the back, right side down, on the front*

twin-needle machine-stitching has been worked inside the lace-insert diamond, 6mm *(¼in)* from the inside edge, and a row of fancy machine embroidery stitching has been worked along the outside edge.

A row of twin-needle machine-stitching and a row of fancy machine embroidery stitching have been worked down the outer edges of the lace C inserted bands.

Making up the pillowcases

Join the short ends of the strips of laces A and B, then gather the straight edge to make a ruffle for each pillowcase (see Lacecraft Techniques 1, page 8).

Pin and then baste the ruffle all round the edges of the pillowcase front (Fig 2).

On each of the pillowcase back pieces, on one short end turn a 6mm *(¼in)* hem and then an 18mm *(¾in)* hem to the wrong side. Machine-stitch and press.

Prepare the inside flap next. On one long side of the flap pieces turn and stitch a double 6mm *(¼in)* hem.

Lay the lace-trimmed pillowcase front right side up. Lay the back on top, right side down, matching all the edges with the pillowcase front except the hemmed edge, which falls short of the front piece (Fig 3). Pin all round except the hemmed end.

Now place the prepared flap right side down so that it overlaps the hemmed end of the back piece (Fig 4). Pin. Baste all round the pillowcase, then machine-stitch through all thicknesses (Fig 5). Trim back the seam allowance to about 6mm *(¼in)* and zigzag-stitch to neaten. Turn pillowcase to right side through flap opening.

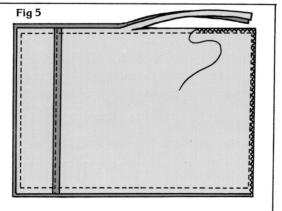

Fig 4 *Place the prepared flap, right side down, on the back piece*

Fig 5 *Machine-stitch all round, trim seam allowance, then zigzag-stitch to neaten*

Crochet and old lace

Many treasured collections of old lace and pieces of crochet are stored away in boxes and drawers and, sadly, are rarely seen.

Carefully used and laundered, old laces do not deteriorate and can have years of useful life, as the original maker intended. By using them for a tablecloth, such as the beautiful damask and lace one pictured, not only will you have created a potential 'family heirloom' but your lace collection can be enjoyed by everyone on special occasions.

Different lace insertion methods have been used to create the tablecloth in the picture and these are described in Lacecraft Techniques 2, page 16.

Conversation piece tablecloth

Materials required

Finished size 1.50m (1⅝yd) square (or to dimensions desired)

1.50m *(1⅝yd)* of 1.50m *(1⅝yd)*-wide damask or cotton fabric (or a purchased, ready-made cloth could be used)*

Lace motifs, edgings, insertions, mats and doilies

Crochet motifs, mats, doilies and pieces

Laundry starch, spray starch

Washable fabric pencil

Rust-proof pins

White blotting paper

*If the lace being used to make the tablecloth is fine and light, use a cotton or lawn fabric rather than damask. Damask is better suited to heavy cotton and crochet laces.

Preparation

By measuring, check that the cut ends of the fabric are straight to the selvedges. Cut off the selvedges. Fold the fabric in half, then quarters and then diagonally, pressing in the creases. Mark the creases with fabric pencil or basting threads.

Wash the pieces of lace and crochet if they are soiled or discoloured (see Caring for Lace, page 16). Make up some strong laundry starch and, while the lace is still wet from washing, dip pieces in the starch. Squeeze out the excess starch and dry the lace flat on blotting paper, gently stretching the pieces back into shape and pinning them out as required.

Spray starch can be used to stiffen lace but you may prefer to use laundry starch on old laces and spray starch on newer laces.

Planning the design

Fig 1 shows the arrangement of laces on the cloth pictured. Your collection of lace and crochet may be very different, so this drawing is only a guide showing how various shapes can be put together for the best effect.

In the middle, a large square lace mat has five doilies sewn to the centre. Spaced around this are four 24cm *(9½in)*-diameter doilies with four L-shaped pieces of insertion between.

A number of scallop-shaped pieces cut from an old, damaged length of lace and small sections of crochet are arranged between the larger units. A length of old, crochet edging encircles the central area.

Large L-shaped pieces are set at the corners, with small doilies positioned in the angles of the L-shapes. Three different patterns of Vandyke-style lace edging are used to finish the hem.

Working the design

Spread the fabric on a large table. Pin the most important piece of lace in the marked centre. Baste this in position, stitching about 15mm *(⅝in)* from the edge. Plan the remainder of the pieces and perhaps make notes, or make a drawing like Fig 1, but it is better to work each piece of lace completely before pinning and basting the next, as starched lace may crease in handling.

Stitching is worked by machine. Depending on the shape and structure of the piece, choose one of the methods suggested under Inserting Lace (see Lacecraft Techniques 2, page 16).

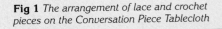

Fig 1 The arrangement of lace and crochet pieces on the Conversation Piece Tablecloth

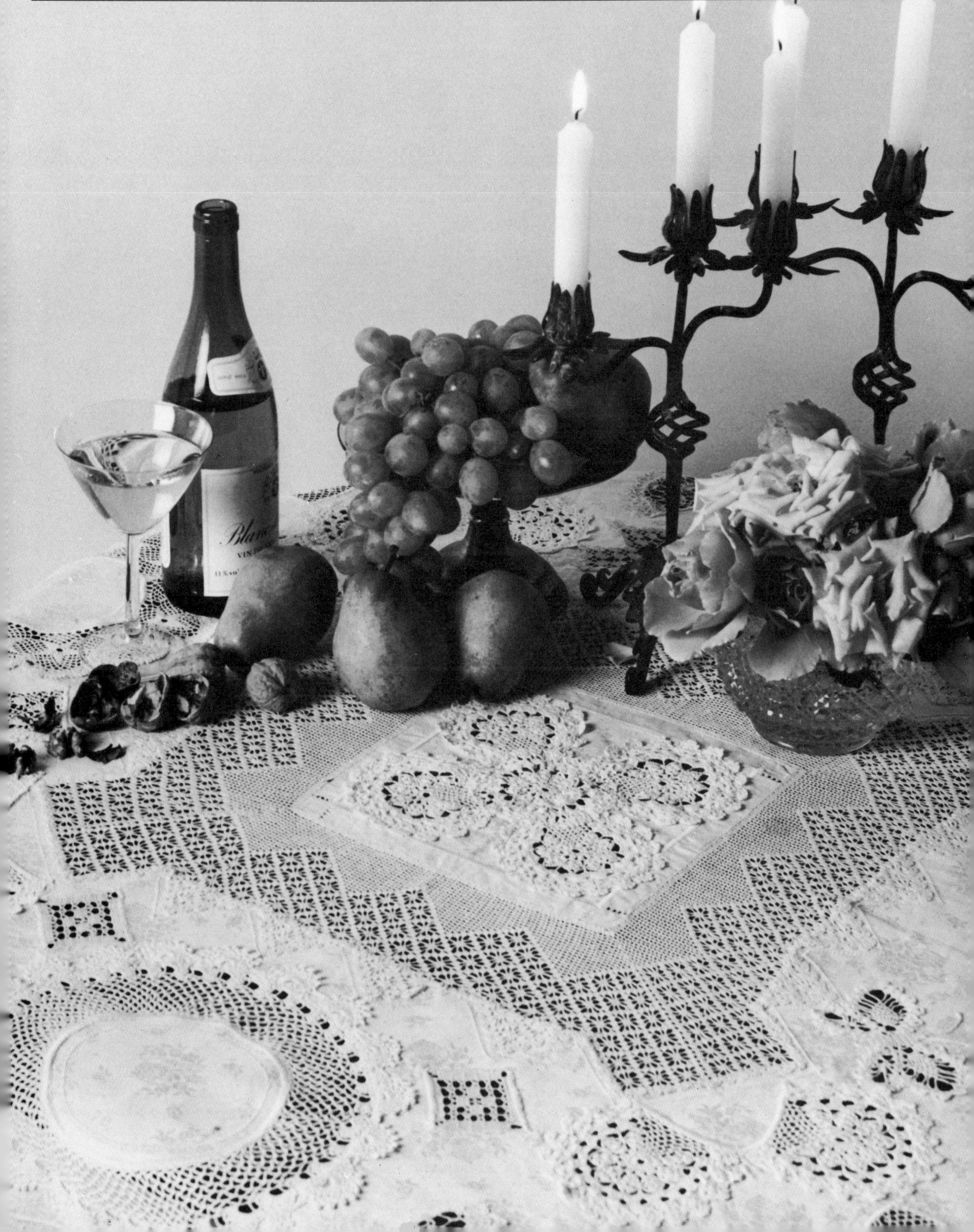

LACECRAFT TECHNIQUES 2

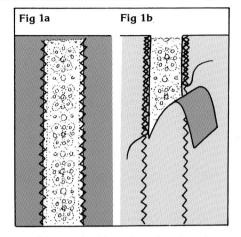

Fig 1a   Fig 1b

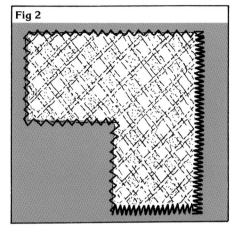

Fig 2

Inserting lace

The techniques described here are used in making the Conversation Piece Tablecloth but they are also used in a variety of other applications, such as for the Romantic Bed Linen (page 12), for making traycloths and napkins, and for decorating blouses and dresses.

Strips There are two kinds of lace strip that can be used for insertion: lace insertion which has two straight edges and galloon which has two decorative edges.

1. Mark the position of the lace strip on the right side of the fabric, then pin and baste down both edges.
2. Working on the right side, with a small zigzag machine-stitch, stitch close to the edges of the lace (Fig 1a). On galloon lace, stitch just inside the decorative edges.
3. On the wrong side, carefully cut away the fabric behind the lace leaving 3mm (⅛in) edges. Depending on the effect you want to achieve on the right side, proceed with one of the following finishes:
4a. Working on the wrong side, work another row of wider zigzag stitch over the cut edges to neaten (Fig 1b).
4b. For a finer finish, sew the cut edges with close whip stitches (see Lacecraft Techniques 1, page 8).
4c. On very fine lace or net, roll the edges of the fabric back and hem, so that no fabric edges show through the lace on the right side.

Insertions on fine fabrics When inserting lace strips or motifs on items made of fine fabric, such as lingerie, a prettier effect will be achieved by working the insertion by hand. Use a fine needle and one strand of

matching embroidery thread and work small whip stitches to apply the lace to the right side of the work. Finish the cut edges on the wrong side with buttonhole stitches.

Small motifs of lace and crochet can be inserted into the corners of handkerchiefs in this way, which is ideal for using precious, tiny pieces of lace.

Shapes with straight edges This technique is used for the L-shaped pieces in the central area and corners of the tablecloth.

1. Pin and baste the piece to the fabric. Work narrow zigzag stitch over the edges of the lace on the right side.
2. Cut away the fabric behind the lace right up to the stitching. Turn to the right side and work zigzag satin stitch over the previous line of zigzag stitches (Fig 2).

Shapes with round or curved edges

1. Pin and baste the piece to the fabric. Straight-stitch round the edges of the lace on the right side, working on a solid area of pattern near to the edge and simplifying the shape as much as possible (Fig 3).
2. On the wrong side, carefully cut away the fabric behind the lace leaving 3mm (⅛in) edges.

3. Spray-starch the edges and press them back right up to the stitching. Work a narrow zigzag stitch with medium spacing over the raw edges to neaten. The stitches must not be too close or the fabric will pucker.
4. On the right side, work a row of tiny straight stitches or a very fine zigzag stitch round the shape. Decorative edges of the shape can be caught down to the fabric if desired.

Inserting damaged doilies and mats

Very pretty effects can be achieved on tablecloths and traycloths by inserting old doilies and mats. Several have been used on the cloth pictured on the previous page.

1. Starch the mats leaving the centre, damaged part intact, and dry flat on blotting paper.
2. Pin and baste the lace mat to the fabric.
3. Work a fine zigzag stitch around the mat, stitching on a solid area of pattern near to the edge.
4. Now work a narrow zigzag stitch around the damaged area in the centre of the mat (Fig 4).
5. On the wrong side, cut away the fabric between the two rows of

---

Caring for lace

Modern lace

Most of the lace trimmings sold in shops are made of nylon, which washes easily, dries quickly and should need no ironing. However, if nylon lace is applied to a garment that needs ironing, great care must be taken to avoid the lace because the heat of the iron will melt the fibres.

Cotton lace is available in both fine, Leavers lace patterns and in Cluny and

Torchon types. Cotton lace washes well but should be pre-shrunk before applying to clothes or linens. Cotton lace is ideal for dyeing with commercial and vegetable dyes (see page 40).

Polyester-cotton laces are completely easy-care, washing well and needing little or no ironing, and are therefore ideal for use on clothing and household linens. Some polyester laces have acetate fibres mixed for a soft handle, and a little care should be taken when ironing these.

Old lace

Old lace can still be found in antique shops and markets and, handled with care, it can be applied to clothing and household linens. Often, old lace is discoloured and will require washing.

White or cream lace Old, machine-made lace should be soaked in cold water for 30 minutes then squeezed twice through warm, soapy water. Rinse well, first in warm water, then cold. Pat dry rolled in a towel. Hang until almost dry before ironing.

Fig 3

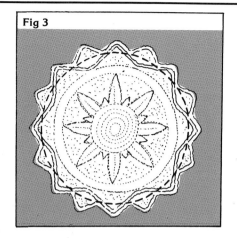

Fig 4

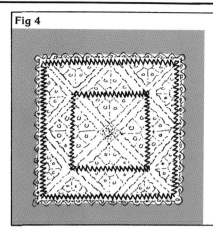

Fig 5

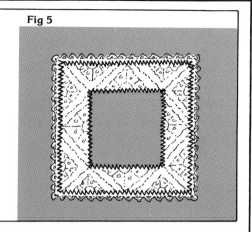

Fig 6

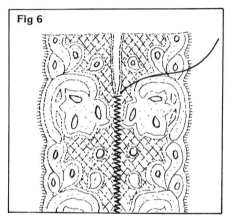

Fig 7

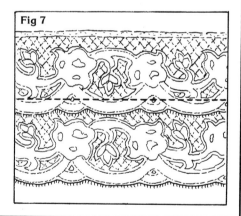

stitching.

6. Work zigzag stitch over the cut edges of the fabric nearest to the outer edges of the mat. (If you prefer, work whip stitching.)

7. On the right side, carefully cut away the area of damaged lace, cutting up to the line of stitches and making sure not to snip into the fabric underneath.

8. Work wider zigzag satin stitch over the line of zigzag stitches (Fig 5).

Motifs from damaged lace

1. Starch the damaged lace and dry flat on blotting paper.

2. Work two rows of machine-stitching all around the good, motif areas.

3. Cut out the motifs close to the stitching.

4. Insert the motifs following the instructions for shapes with round or curved edges.

Joining lace edge to edge

Lace edging can be joined to insertion or beading to make a wider strip than may be available.

1. Spray-starch and press both pieces of cotton lace to be joined.

2. Place the two pieces together right sides up, butting the edges. They should not overlap.

3. Zigzag-stitch the two edges together, using No. 50 machine embroidery cotton thread and setting the stitch just wide enough to catch in the headings of the laces (Fig 6). Start about 6–9mm (¼ – ⅜in) from the end so that the lace does not become caught in the machine's feed teeth.

4. Press the lace and work a slightly wider zigzag stitch over the seam again from the other side.

Joining lace edging

Strips of lace edging can be joined together to make a wide strip. This is a useful technique if a wide lace ruffle is required for a hem with a matching, narrower lace for necklines or sleeves.

Galloon lace can be joined each side of insertion or beading using this technique.

1. Spray-starch and press the cotton lace.

2. Arrange two strips of edging so that the decorative edge of one overlaps the straight edge of the other. Try to arrange the pattern so that motifs are aligned, or so that they make a decorative effect.

3. Set the sewing-machine to a medium-length straight stitch. Stitch just inside the straight edge of the lower piece of edging (Fig 7).

Hand-made lace If it is reasonably strong, wash and dry as described for machine-made lace. If the lace is fine and perhaps damaged, baste white fabric round a bottle, wind the lace round and, holding the bottle in one hand, wash in warm, soapy water.

Another method, which is rather safer for fragile lace, involves putting the lace into a bottle of warm, soapy water and shaking the bottle until the dirt washes out.

If stains persist, lace may be boiled, but put it first into a cotton bag.

Black lace Soak black lace in cold tea for 30 minutes, then squeeze and soak again in cool tea mixed with a little liquid soap. Rinse in cool tea. If the lace is to be stiffened, add a teaspoon of gum water to the last rinsing (one teaspoon of gum arabic crystals to a large cup of water).

Mending lace

Lace can be mended by the same method as joining lace (see Lacecraft Techniques 2). Baste the lace over blue paper for working.

Ironing lace

Ironing lace tends to flatten the raised pattern. If possible, dry lace flat, pulling it gently into shape and pinning out with rust-proof pins. If ironing is necessary, work on a soft, padded surface, with the lace right side down, and place a piece of kitchen paper between the iron and the lace.

Lace and Needlework

Fine hand-work is enhanced with a touch of luxurious lace. In this chapter, favourite needlework techniques — soft box-making, beading, appliqué, embroidery on tulle and net, and shadow embroidery — take on a new dimension when worked with lace.

Jewel box in lace

Materials required

Finished size 16 × 24 × 9.5cm
(6¼ × 9¼ × 3¾in)
80 × 75cm *(31 × 30in)* soft plain fabric
80 × 75cm *(31 × 30in)* medium-weight interfacing
80 × 38cm *(31 × 15in)* all-over lace
1.40m *(1½yd)* of 5cm *(2in)*-wide lace edging
Sheet of thin card
All-purpose clear adhesive

Preparation

Cut pieces of card as follows and mark to identify them as instructed.
Two pieces 16 × 24cm *(6¼ × 9¼in)*. Mark one piece Top Outer A, the other Bottom Outer B.
Two pieces 3mm *(⅛in)* smaller all round. Mark one piece Top Lining a, the other Bottom Lining b.
Two pieces 9.5 × 24cm *(3¾ × 9¼in)*. Mark each Long Side Outer C.
Two pieces 3mm *(⅛in)* smaller all round. Mark each Long Side Lining c.
Two pieces 9.5 × 16cm *(3¾ × 6¼in)*. Mark each Short Side Outer D.
Two pieces 3mm *(⅛in)* smaller all round. Mark each Short Side Lining d.

Cut pieces of interfacing to the same sizes plus 9mm *(⅜in)* all round. Cut fabric to the same sizes plus 12mm *(½in)* all round.

Cut all-over lace for pieces A, B, C and D (the outer box pieces) to the same size as the fabric for these pieces.

Working the design

Cover each piece of card with interfacing, folding the edges over to the other side and glueing them down. Leave to dry under weights (books will do).

When dry, cover the interfacing with the fabric pieces, folding the edges over to the wrong side and glueing down. Leave to dry under weights.

Cover pieces A, B, C and D with the all-over lace, mounting the lace over the fabric side of the cards and glueing down on·the wrong side. Leave to dry.

Assembling the box

Gather the lace edging with tiny stitches. Neaten the cut ends of the lace with oversewing. Sew the lace round the box lid (piece A) on one long side and two short sides, working on the wrong side of the lid 3mm *(⅛in)* inside the edge. Use hemming stitches. Press gathers where stitched.

Glue the lining pieces to the outer pieces, card sides together. Centre the lining pieces on the outers for all sections of the box.

Join the box pieces together with hand-sewing. Using matching thread, oversew the two long sides and the two short sides to the box base, then sew the box corners together. (Embroidery stitches, such as Cretan stitch, may be used instead of oversewing, if preferred.)

Oversew the lid to the back edge of the box. If preferred, a loop and button fastener can be sewn to the lid and the box. Alternatively, sew ribbons to the lid and the box and tie in a bow. Decorate the box lid if required with beading (see page 20) or embroidery.

Beading on lace

If you have never tried beading, working on lace is a good way to begin this fascinating and rewarding needlecraft. The pattern of the lace provides lines on which to work and the finished beadwork can have many uses — as decorative panels on fashion clothes, collars and cuffs, on belts and bags, or to make a beautiful keepsake, such as the wedding album cover in the picture.

Tools and materials

Lace The heavier the lace, the easier it is to bead. Guipure motifs or all-over lace adapts best to the techniques of beading but fine laces can also be worked if the lace is mounted on fabric to provide sufficient weight and support.

Threads No. 50 sewing cotton thread is ideal for beading. Choose a colour to match the ground fabric and to harmonize with the beads. Pull cotton thread over a piece of beeswax or candle wax to smooth the thread and strengthen it for working. Invisible nylon thread can be used on fine nets and tulles.

Needles Beading needles are very fine and long and suited to the craft. Ordinary, slim sewing needles may be used but make sure that the threaded needle will pass easily through all the different types of beads.

Choosing beads

The range of beads available is vast and it is all too easy to make the mistake of choosing several different types for a design. You will find it simpler to work a design if you limit your selection to about four types: three styles in the same colour range but in different shapes and one entirely different type of bead or sequin.

For instance, round pearl beads, flat pearly flowers and white crystal beads contrasting with silver sequins would make an effective range to work with.

Preparation

All-over guipure lace can be put direct into an embroidery frame for working but take care not to tear the lace when fastening the frame.

Finer laces should be basted on to a background fabric before being put into an embroidery frame, and the

Beading techniques

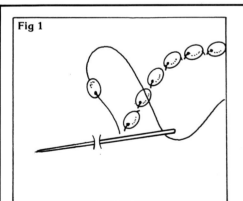

Six methods of attaching beads and sequins to fabric are shown. Start with a double backstitch on the wrong side of the work and finish in the same way. Do not draw threads up too tightly or the work will pucker. Beadwork should not be pressed but if it is absolutely necessary, press on the wrong side working on a pad or folded towel and avoid pressing over the beads or they may break.

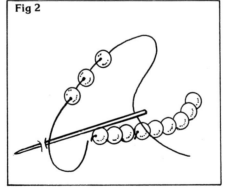

Scatter effects (Fig 1)

Each bead is attached individually. Bring the needle through to the front of the work and pick up one bead. Slide it along the needle and just on to the thread, then pick up one thread of the background fabric the length of the bead along the design line. Draw the thread through to position the bead, then pick up the next bead on the needle.

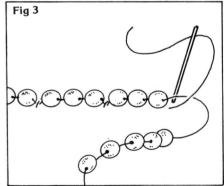

Straight lines (Fig 2)

Bring the needle through to the front of the work and pick up three or four beads. Slide them just on to the thread. Make a single running stitch, which positions the needle for the next group of beads to be picked up.

Curved lines (Fig 3)

Two needles and thread are used at the same time. Thread beads on to needle and thread 1. Needle and thread 2 is used to make a couching stitch between groups of beads.

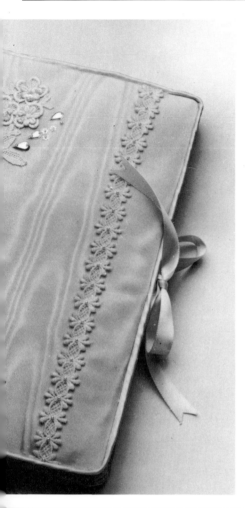

beading is worked through both layers.

Baste guipure motifs on a background fabric and then put the fabric into the frame.

The album cover in the picture has polyester wadding backing the fabric, which provided sufficient weight for the fabric to be worked without the use of an embroidery frame.

Beadwork on the wedding album pictured (half the design is shown):
A *Half pearl bead glued down*
B *Diamante stone glued down*
C *Flower-shaped pearl bead with crystal bead stitched through. The centre is a flat pearl bead with a crystal bead stitched through*
D *A half pearl bead is glued in the centre and surrounded with tiny pearl beads stitched through lace. Pearlised sequins are stitched to the centre of the petals*
E *Crystal beads are stitched to opalescent drops and to flower-shaped pearl beads. Tiny pearls and silver sequins make up the group*
F *A large pearl bead in the centre is surrounded by small pearl beads stitched through large octagonal crystal beads. Petals are filled with crystal beads and with small crystal beads stitched through flower-shaped pearl beads*
G *Crystal beads stitched through pearlised sequins*

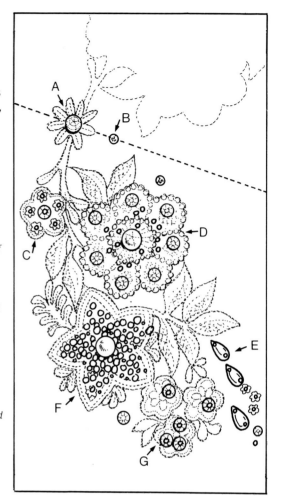

Fig 4

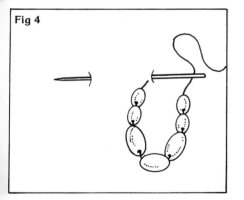

Fig 5

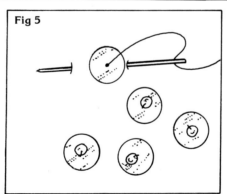

Fig 6

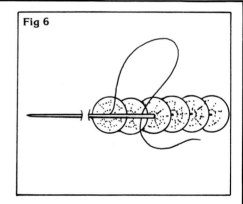

Bead loops (Fig 4)
This technique can be used for decorative effects or as an edging.

Bring the needle through from the wrong side of the work and pick up sufficient beads to make the loop required. Pick up a thread of the fabric to secure the loop, ready for the next bead or beads.

Loops of beads can be fastened to the centre of a circle to make daisy effects, the petals lying free of the background fabric.

Scatter sequins (Fig 5)
Single sequins can be attached in two ways. In method 1, bring the needle through from the wrong side, pass it through the sequin and then make a backstitch through the fabric. The sequin lies flat on the fabric and the needle is in position for the next sequin.

In method 2, bring the needle through from the wrong side, pass it through the sequin and then through a small bead. Pass the needle back through the hole in the sequin and

finish off the thread with a backstitch on the wrong side.

When attaching scatter sequins to lace or net, work several oversewing stitches round a single thread of the lace or net.

Scale effects (Fig 6)
Bring the needle up through the hole in the sequin, set the sequin on the design line, then take a small stitch to the side of the sequin. Slip the next sequin on to the needle and do the same again.

Dream roses pillow

Shadow appliqué, lustrous satin ribbon and crisp broderie anglaise edging combine to make this charming pillow.

Materials required

Finished size (without ruffle)
28×34cm (11×13½in)
40cm (16in) of 120cm (48in)-wide
   white cotton organdie
40cm (16in) of 120cm (48in)-wide
   white polycotton fabric for backing
2m (2¼yd) of 5cm (2in)-wide
   broderie anglaise edging
1.40m (1½yd) of 15mm (⅝in)-wide
   broderie anglaise beading
1.40m (1½yd) of 6mm (¼in)-wide
   double face satin ribbon
30cm (12in) squares cotton fabric for
   appliqué in red, dark, medium and
   light pinks, dark and light greens
6 pieces 30cm (12in) square
   lightweight iron-on interfacing
Stranded embroidery threads in
   dark, medium and light pinks,
   dark and light greens
Small amount of medium green
   tapestry wool
Cushion pad
Blunt-tipped needle, embroidery
   needle
Paste in solid stick form
Squared pattern paper, 1sq=2.5cm
   (1in)
Tracing paper

Preparation

Draw the pattern (Fig 1) up to full size on squared pattern paper. Draw the outlines firmly. Trace off on to tracing paper to make the appliqué patterns.

From organdie cut a piece 31×37cm (12×14½in) for the embroidery. Cut a piece the same size from the cotton backing.

For the back of the pillow cut pieces of organdie and cotton to the same size as the front. Baste them together round the edges and then from corner to corner diagonally to hold the pieces firmly together during working.

Pin the backing fabric for the embroidery to the drawing on squared pattern paper. If the lines show through fairly clearly this will be sufficient guide for placing the appliqué pieces. If the lines are indistinct tape the pattern and fabric to a window and trace the pattern lines on to the fabric.

Iron the interfacing to the wrong side of the red, pink and green appliqué fabrics. Cut the tracing paper pattern into pieces and, following the graph pattern (Fig 1), use the pieces to cut shapes from the red, pink and green fabrics. No turnings are necessary. Tiny pieces, such as the centres of roses, are easier to cut freehand.

As pieces are cut, unpin the paper patterns and paste each in position on the cotton fabric, overlapping edges a little where shapes meet. Very small shapes are placed on top of larger pieces. Lay the organdie over the work, matching fabric edges. Baste the layers together round the outside edges.

Working the design

Using two strands of thread in the embroidery needle, work running stitches round the shapes through both thicknesses of fabric, matching thread colours to fabrics.

When changing thread colours, knot the thread end and bring the needle through from the back. To finish thread ends, work a backstitch on the wrong side of work through the backing fabric.

Working from the picture, add petals to the roses and veins to the leaves. For the stems, work two rows of running stitches 3mm (⅛in) apart.

To complete the shadow appliqué, thread the blunt-tipped needle with green tapestry wool and, working on the wrong side of the work, push the needle through the backing fabric and thread the wool along the main stems. Leave about 12mm (½in) of wool hanging at beginning and end without knotting.

Finishing

Join the ends of the broderie anglaise edging with a straight seam and press the seam open. Neaten the edges with zigzag stitch.

Gather the straight edge and fit the ruffle round the piece of embroidery, matching straight edges of ruffle and fabric. Pin and then baste. Machine-stitch the ruffle to the pillow piece. Remove basting threads.

Make up the pillow as for a cushion (see page 8), inserting a zip into one of the side seams. Remove basting threads from the back.

Thread the ribbon through the broderie anglaise beading. Hand-sew the beading to the pillow, following the picture and neatly mitring the corners (see page 9 for technique). Tie the ends of the ribbon in a bow at one corner.

Fig 1 *Graph pattern for Dream Roses shadow appliqué, 1sq = 2.5cm (1in)*

Key to colours
□ red
○ light pink
✕ medium pink
■ dark pink
● light green
▲ dark green

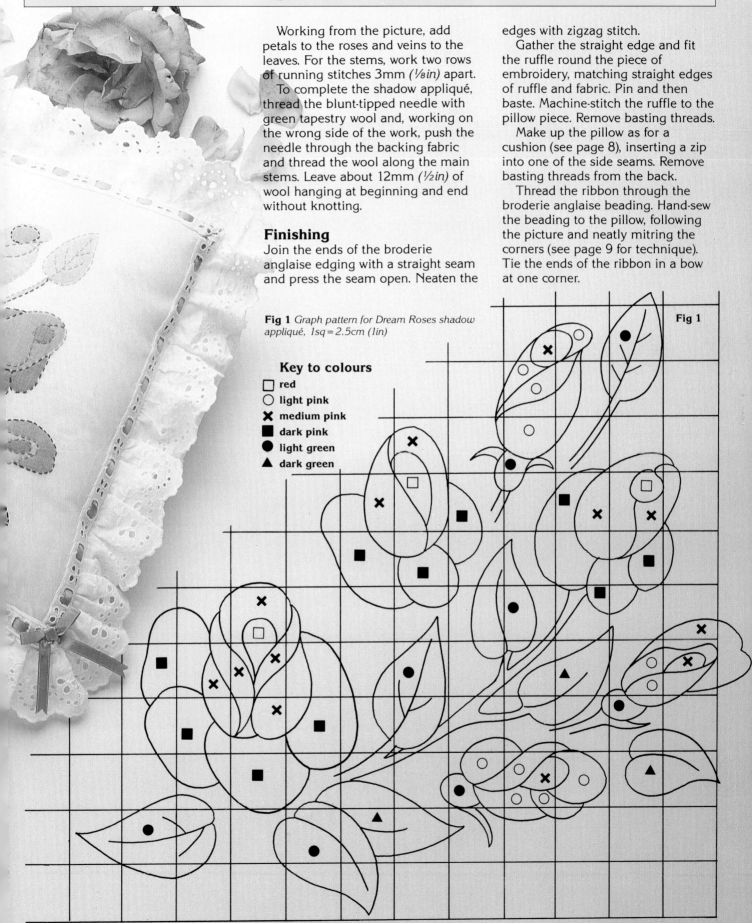

Fig 1

Lace appliqué cushions

Lace appliqué can produce different effects depending on the type of lace used and the techniques involved. The two cushions pictured use guipure and organdie motifs, chosen to make flower and leaf garlands. Some of the petals and leaves are left free of the background fabric, giving an extra dimension to the needlework.

Both cushions are made on the same basic design – a central hexagon of ribbons surrounding a circlet of flowers, with garlands of flowers and leaves grouped around the hexagon. Use washable fabrics to make the cushions and pre-shrink guipure and organdie motifs, so that the finished cushions can be home-laundered.

Fig 1 *Pencil round the paper circle on the satin fabric square and mark the six points*

Fig 2 *Baste and stitch the strips of ribbon round the marked circle*

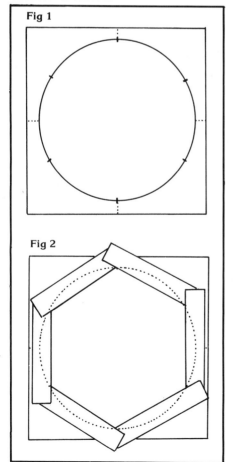

White lace garland cushion

Materials required

Finished size (without ruffle) 38cm (15in) square
50cm *(20in)* of 120cm *(48in)*-wide white polyester satin fabric
50cm *(20in)* of 120cm *(48in)*-wide white embroidered net fabric
4 large guipure or organdie motifs
8 each of three different guipure motifs
3.75m *(4⅛yd)* of 18mm *(¾in)*-wide white double face satin ribbon
1.60m *(1¾yd)* of 18mm *(¾in)*-wide white textured ribbon
2.50m *(2¾yd)* of 10cm *(4in)*-wide lace edging
Cushion pad
Pattern paper
Pair of compasses

Preparation

Cut a 20cm *(8in)* square from the satin fabric and mark the middle by creasing both ways. Draw a circle on paper with a 9cm *(3½in)* radius. Using the compasses, mark six points on the circumference of the circle at regular intervals. Cut out the paper circle and pin it to the centre of the satin square. Pencil round the circle on the fabric and mark in the six points (Fig 1).

Cut six pieces of the textured ribbon 14cm *(5½in)* long and six pieces 11cm *(4½in)* long. Cut six pieces of satin ribbon 12.5cm *(5in)* long and four pieces 38cm *(15in)* long.

From the satin fabric cut two pieces 40cm *(16in)* square. Cut a piece of embroidered net to the same size. Join the ends of the lace

edging (see Lacecraft Techniques 1, page 8).

Working the design
Baste the six shorter strips of textured ribbon round the marked circle on the satin square (Fig 2). Machine-stitch on the inner edge. Baste the six shorter strips of white satin ribbon next, overlapping the first row of ribbons by about half. Machine-stitch on the inner edge. Baste the remaining six textured ribbon strips in the same way, to form the third, outer row. Machine-stitch on both edges.

Pin and baste the net to the right side of one satin piece. Baste the four long strips of satin ribbon to the edges and then machine-stitch on the inside edge using a wide zigzag machine-stitch or any decorative machine embroidery stitch.

Hand-appliqué a circle of flower motifs to the centre of the hexagon.

Trim the satin square back to within 6mm (¼in) of the hexagon edges. Turn the satin edge under, baste and then zigzag-stitch the hexagon to the middle of the net-covered cushion piece.

Arrange the lace motifs around the hexagon. Place the four large motifs at the corners and the rest in between, to create a natural flow of flowers and leaves. There need not be symmetry in the arrangement.

Hand-sew the motifs to the cushion piece, taking tiny stitches on the edges of the motifs and through the fabric background. Work some of the stitches inside the edges of the motifs so that the edges are slightly free of the background. Do not press the finished work.

Finishing
Gather the lace edging for the cushion ruffle (see Lacecraft Techniques 1, page 8) and make up the cushion cover (see also page 8).

Make small stitched bows from the remaining white satin ribbon and sew over 10cm (4in) fish-tailed ends at the corners (see picture).

Tan and ecru cushion
Four different toning ribbons are used, as follows: 2.50m (2¾yd) white satin ribbon; 2.15m (2⅜yd) tan satin ribbon; 1.20m (1⅜yd) cream satin ribbon; 75cm (30in) cream textured ribbon.

The guipure and organdie motifs grouped in the hexagon centre and round the edges, on cream embroidered net fabric, are in a variety of tan shades, to tone with the ribbons.

More ideas for lace appliqué
Lace appliqué, where a variety of motifs and shapes are sewn to a background fabric to make a design, lends itself to many uses in home furnishings and also to fashion. The sprays built up on the Tan and Ecru Cushion, for instance, would look superb worked on a satin bedspread. A single spray could be applied to the top of a soft jewellery box for a dressing-table accessory (Fig 1) and the same motif worked on a matching organdie runner.

For fashion work, a large area of applied lace and ribbons could be used on the back of an evening coat. Smaller appliquéd sprays or motifs could be sewn to the shoulder of a knitted sweater or cardigan.

Fig 1

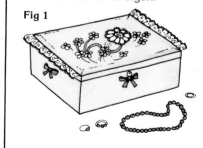

LACECRAFT TECHNIQUES 3

Motifs from lace

Motifs cut from all-over lace can be used to embellish wedding clothes, evening wear, lingerie and decorative children's wear, and can look luxurious applied to hand-made bed linen.

1. Cut motifs from all-over lace, allowing 2.5cm (1in) all round.
2. Position the motifs on the background fabric, using stick adhesive on net or tulle fabrics and fine pins on other, woven fabrics.
3. Motifs can be applied to fabric by hand or by machine. Using hand-sewing, work tiny whip stitches on the edges of the motifs (see Lacecraft Techniques 1, page 8). To machine-stitch, set the work in an embroidery hoop and use a medium-size stitch just inside motif edges.
4. When sewing is completed, trim away excess fabric around the motifs.

Joining all-over lace

Pieces of all-over lace fabric or lengths of wide lace edging are joined with an appliqué technique. Either hand-sewing or machine-stitching can be used and, properly done, the finished join is virtually invisible.

1. Overlap the two pieces of lace, matching the pattern on the upper and lower layers, and pin together.
2. Working by hand, whip stitch around the edges of the motif on the upper layer, stitching through to the motif on the lower layer (Fig 1).
3. Working by machine, first baste the two layers together, then stitch around the outline of the upper layer motif using a narrow zigzag stitch.
4. After stitching, trim away the excess fabric on both layers, close to the stitching.

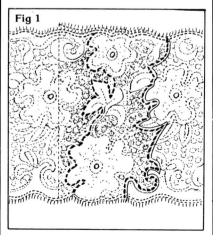

Fig 1

Lace fascinator

Lace motifs are not always easily available but if an all-over lace fabric with a distinct pattern can be obtained, a short length will provide you with a number of motifs that can be cut out and used for appliqué.

The 'fascinator' shawl in the picture is made of cream spotted tulle appliquéd with motifs cut from Chantilly lace in a similar colour. The shaped border is made by 'invisibly' joining pieces of the same Chantilly lace. The technique of joining all-over lace is useful to learn and enables an expensive lace to be used more economically.

The technique for applying sequins to lace can be found on page 21. Alternatively, sequins can be applied with a touch of clear adhesive.

Materials required

Finished size 160cm (63in) on longest edge, 63cm (25in) at deepest point
60cm (24in) of 120cm (48in)-wide cream tulle
60cm (24in) of 120cm (48in)-wide all-over cream Chantilly lace with large motifs
3m (3¼yd) of 10cm (4in)-wide cream lace edging
3m (3¼yd) of 1.5mm (¹⁄₁₆in)-wide cream satin ribbon
7 lace butterfly motifs (optional)
1 packet of small pearlised sequins (optional)
Paste in solid stick form

Preparation

Fold the tulle across the width. Measure and cut the fascinator (Fig 1). From the remaining tulle (shaded in Fig 1), cut three strips across the width 2.5cm (1in) wide.

From the Chantilly lace cut one strip across the width 15cm (6in) deep and then another strip to the same depth and about 66–71cm (26–28in) wide. These two pieces are to be joined at the ends, so it is important that the motifs on the ends match. Choose the area from which you will cut the second strip to achieve a matching motif.

From the remaining Chantilly lace cut out several motifs allowing approximately 2.5cm (1in) all round.

At the turn of the century, lace fascinators were worn to cover the shoulders or as an evening head-covering

Fig 1 *Fold the tulle and cut out the fascinator on the fold*

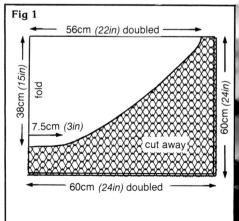

Fig 1

56cm (22in) doubled

38cm (15in)

fold

7.5cm (3in)

cut away

60cm (24in)

60cm (24in) doubled

Working the design

Position the motifs on the tulle working to within 2.5cm (*1in*) of the curved edge (see picture). Hold the motifs in position temporarily with a dab of adhesive. Stitch the motifs to the tulle (see Lacecraft Techniques 3).

Join the two strips of Chantilly lace (see Lacecraft Techniques 3), to make a strip 183cm (*72in*) long. With right sides together, pin and baste the Chantilly strip 6mm (*¼in*) inside the curved edge of the tulle, working from both ends towards the centre. Gather the middle 66cm (*26in*) and then finish pinning and basting the strip around the curved point of the fascinator.

Set the sewing-machine to a narrow zigzag stitch and stitch the Chantilly lace to the tulle, first right sides together and then on the right side, working over the seam again.

Gather the lace edging (see Lacecraft Techniques 1, page 8). Baste the gathered lace along the bottom edge of the Chantilly lace strip, wrong side of lace edging to the right side of Chantilly lace, then topstitch using zigzag machine-stitching.

Join the three 2.5cm (*1in*)-wide strips of tulle on the short ends with zigzag stitch. Neaten both long edges of the strip with zigzag stitch. Machine-gather down the centre.

Baste the gathered strip over the join between the main fascinator piece and the Chantilly lace strip, and along the straight edge. Set the machine to a wide zigzag stitch. Stitch the gathered strip working over the gathering line and catching in the narrow ribbon as you stitch. (Lay the ribbon on the seam line under the machine's presser foot and position the ribbon while stitching. If preferred, the ribbon can be couched down by hand after stitching down the gathered strip.)

Finishing

Catch the lace butterfly motifs to the tulle, leaving the wing tips free of the fabric. Sew sequins at random over the lace motifs, on the gathered frill and along the hem (see picture). Alternatively, attach sequins with a touch of clear adhesive.

Embroidery on tulle

Tulle embroidery looks like lace and this delicate work can be used to make a wedding veil or perhaps an overdress for a baby gown. Mounted over a solid-colour fabric, tulle embroidery makes exquisite cushions.

The lovebirds and heart motif pictured could be repeated around the hem of a short or long veil, as shown on page 53, or it could be used on the ends of an evening scarf.

Small pieces of embroidery are worked in an embroidery hoop but for large pieces, such as a veil, the tulle is mounted over architects' tracing linen and the work supported on a table top.

Pearl cotton, lace thread and stranded embroidery threads are all suitable for tulle embroidery. Needles should be blunt-tipped and pass easily through the holes in the tulle.

The basic stitches used in this embroidery are Running stitch, worked vertically, horizontally or diagonally, Stem stitch, Cording, and Darning stitch, with Buttonhole stitch used for edges. There are several filling stitches that are used for this work and some of them are based on ordinary embroidery stitches. Three are used in the lovebirds and heart motif: Wave stitch, Lattice Filling and Star Filling.

Lovebirds and heart

Materials required
Finished motif size (without scalloped edge) 15×20cm (6×8in)
40cm *(16in)* square silk or nylon tulle
White stranded embroidery thread
Tracing paper
Soft, dark blue paper (or other dark colour)
White watercolour paint and brush, or white pencil
Blunt-tipped needle
Embroidery hoop*

Preparation
Trace the half-motif (Fig 1) on folded tracing paper, then re-trace the lines to obtain the whole motif as shown in the picture. Lay the tracing on the blue paper and draw over the lines with a hard pencil, pressing firmly to mark the lines on the surface of the blue paper. Draw over the pressed marks with white paint or white pencil.

Baste the tulle over the design, making sure that a straight line of mesh holes runs down the centre of the heart. Place the mounted tulle in the embroidery hoop.
*If an embroidery hoop is not available, the mounted tulle can be basted to a piece of lightweight card, which will support the embroidery adequately.

Working the design
To secure thread ends in tulle embroidery, the doubled thread is looped under a thread of the tulle and then the needle is passed back through the loop and the embroidery thread pulled tight (Fig 2). Long ends are left on the wrong side of the work and darned in after the embroidery is completed.

Outline the birds and the heart first in Running stitch using six strands of thread in the needle. Do not work the wing and tail feathers at this stage.

The birds' breasts are worked in Darning stitch, using two strands of thread. Pass the needle in and out of mesh holes, going over, under, over, under tulle threads on the first row, then work a second row back in the same holes, going under threads where before you went over, and over where you went under. Follow the picture for shaping the Darning stitch area.

Work Wave stitch on the birds' wings and tails, using one strand of thread (Fig 3). Work Lattice Filling on the heart, using two strands of thread (Fig 4). Now work the wing and tail feathers in Running stitch, using six strands of thread. The birds' eyes and the flowers in the background are Star Fillings, using two strands of thread (Fig 5). The birds' beaks are worked with a few straight stitches, using one strand of thread.

The sprays of leaves under the birds are worked in Running stitch,

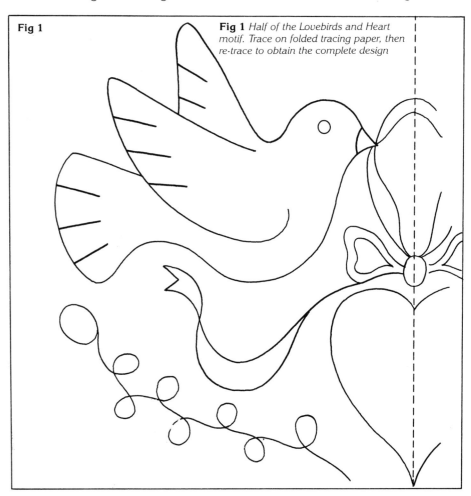

Fig 1 Half of the Lovebirds and Heart motif. Trace on folded tracing paper, then re-trace to obtain the complete design

using two strands of thread. (Try to work an entire spray with one length, avoiding joins which would show.)

The 'ribbon' strands trailing from the heart and the ribbon loop and bow between the birds are also worked in Running stitch, using one strand of thread. The picots surrounding the heart are worked with a single strand of thread.

Finishing

Outline the scallops with Running stitch, using six strands of thread. Then work Buttonhole stitch over the Running stitches, and another row of Running stitch just inside the scallops, both with three strands of thread.

Cut away the tulle close to the scallops. Unpick the basting stitches to remove the tulle embroidery from the pattern and darn in any thread ends on the back of the work.

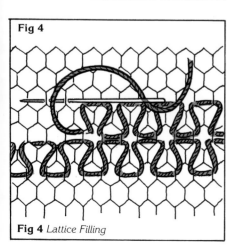

Fig 2 To secure thread ends, loop doubled thread under a mesh thread, pass the needle back through the loop and pull thread tight

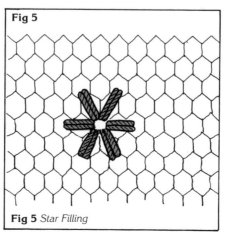

Fig 3 Wave stitch

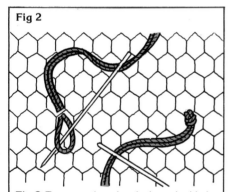

Fig 4 Lattice Filling

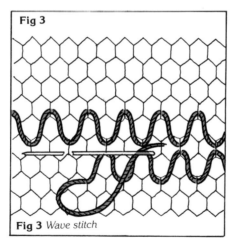

Fig 5 Star Filling

Making a wedding veil

For both short and long veils, tulle should be 1.85m (2yd) wide and you will need two separate lengths folded to make four layers.

For a short veil, measure from the crown of the head to the elbow and double the measurement. Buy two separate lengths to this measurement. Fold the two lengths in half across the width and work two rows of Running stitch along the fold, pulling them up to fit the veil on to the head-dress. A single layer of tulle is thrown forward over the face.

For a long veil, measure from the crown of the head to the floor and add the measurement from the crown to the elbow. You need two lengths of the total measurement. Round off the corners of both lengths. Fold them together across the width, at the crown to elbow measurement. Find the centre point on the fold. Mark a point 15cm (6in) each side of the centre and work Running stitch along this central 30cm (12in). Pull up the gathers to fit the head-dress.

The cut edges of tulle veils can be left unfinished, but a simple edging embroidery looks more professional.

Machine embroidery on net

Decorative lace effects can be produced by the technique of machine embroidery on net fabric. The silver stars on the evening top pictured are worked in straight stitch but the Lurex thread is wound on to the bobbin of the machine and the embroidery is worked from the wrong side.

Silver-starred top

Materials required

Finished size: bust 86cm (34in); shoulder to hem 50cm (20in)
60cm *(24in)* of 120cm *(48in)*-wide black spotted net or tulle
60cm *(24in)* of 120cm *(48in)*-wide black georgette or similar fabric for lining
50m *(55yd)* spool silver Lurex machine thread, black thread, white basting thread
4m *(4⅜yd)* silver crochet or knitting yarn
10 large sequins, 25 medium-sized sequins, 50 small sequins
All-purpose clear adhesive (or tiny glass beads)
Squared pattern paper, 1sq=5cm *(2in)*
Large machine needle for embroidery (size 100/16)
Embroidery hoop

Preparation

Draw the pattern (Fig 1) up to full size on squared pattern paper. Mark the centre Front and centre Back to be placed to fold of fabric as shown. Cut out the two pattern pieces.

Cut the net and lining fabric down the middle so that you have two net pieces 60cm *(24in)* square and two lining pieces of the same size. Fold each net piece in half so that the fold is parallel with the selvedges. Pin all round the edges.

Pin the pattern pieces for Front and Back on the net, to the fold as indicated on the pattern. Work running stitch with white basting thread all around the pattern pieces,

including the scallops, through one layer of net. Unpin the pattern carefully, re-pin to the other side of the folded fabric and outline the pattern again, to give the complete Front and Back.

Unpin the patterns and work the lining pieces in the same way.

Cut out the lining pieces, cutting 9mm *(⅜in)* from the line of running stitches. Do not cut out the scallops at this stage. Do not cut out the net pieces until the embroidery is completed.

Wind the silver Lurex machine thread on to the bobbin. Insert the large machine needle and thread the machine with black thread. Loosen the top tension just a little and test the stitch on a piece of scrap net and lining.

The large stars in the scallops are worked first so put the net fabric into the embroidery hoop, right side down, ready to work the stars in this area. (Bind the hoop sections with tape if it helps to hold the net more firmly.)

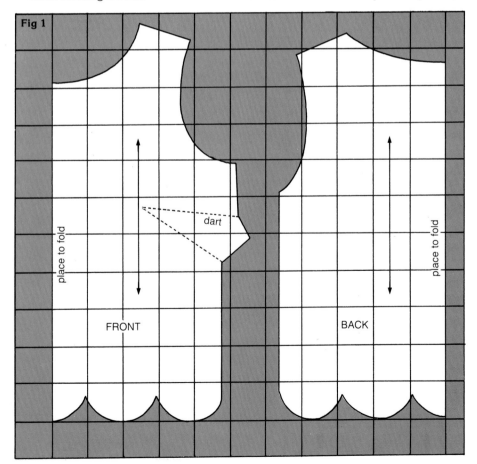

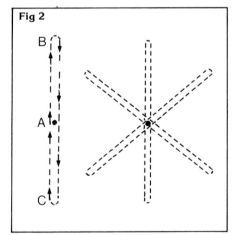

Fig 1 *Graph pattern for the Silver-starred Top, 1sq=5cm (2in)*

Fig 2 *Work stars from the wrong side of fabric. Stitch from the middle of the star A forward to point B, back to C and forward to A. You are now in position to work the next point*

Right, the scalloped hem of the Silver-starred Top falls just above hip level. The length can be extended to below the hip – or further – by adjusting the pattern on the line of squares just above the scallops

Working the embroidery

The large stars are formed with four intersecting lines, each one worked with two double rows of stitching. The smaller stars have three intersecting lines, each worked with one double row of stitching.

Start and finish in the middle of each star (Fig 2). Do not worry if the stitching looks uneven — the effect will be more spontaneous. Position the stars at random on Front and Back net pieces (see picture).

Making up the top

When all the embroidery is completed, cut out the net Front and Back, cutting 9mm (⅜in) from the line of white running stitches.

Re-adjust the machine for normal stitching. Stitch the darts on the Front, trim the seam to 6mm (¼in) and oversew or zigzag-stitch to neaten. Work the darts on the lining Front in the same way.

Pin and baste the net and lining Fronts together, right sides facing. Pin the darts together. Baste along the scallops, just outside the line of running stitches. Machine-stitch the scallops, the neckline and around the armholes, stitching just inside the line of running stitches, then unpick all white threads. Snip into curves. Trim the seam allowances to 6mm (¼in) and neaten. Work the Back in the same way. Turn Front and Back to right side.

Place Front and Back together, right sides facing, then baste and stitch shoulder and side seams. Trim seam allowances and neaten. Turn to right side and press lightly.

Finishing

Work narrow zigzag stitching around the armholes on the right side. Stitch the silver yarn around the neckline and scallops with zigzag stitch.

Glue large sequins on to the large stars and medium-sized sequins on to the stars around the waistline. Use the small sequins on the stars near to the top of the garment. Glued-on sequins will stay in place in normal wearing but may drop off in dry cleaning. If you prefer, sew the sequins in position with the tiny glass beads (see the techniques for attaching scatter sequins described on page 21).

Lace and Crafts

Lace can be used with other materials in a great variety of crafts to add a touch of prettiness — or whimsy, as on the Flight of Birds mobile (page 38). Lace also has its own range of crafts, for flower-making, picture-making, jewellery-making or, stiffened with sugar, for making baskets for sweets or flowers.

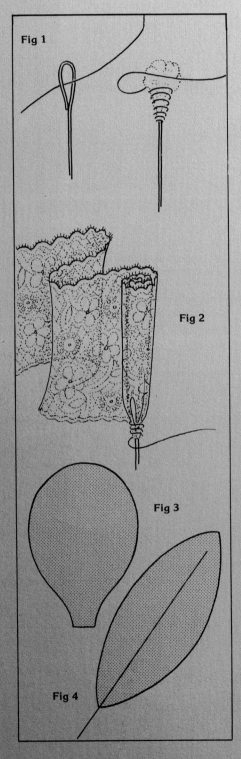

Fig 1

Fig 2

Fig 3

Fig 4

Lace flowers

Flowers can be made from all kinds of material, including paper, feathers, ribbons and silk fabrics, but lace produces an entirely different effect — formal yet fragile.

Cotton lace can be tinted with watercolour or fabric paints, but white or cream arrangements have a charm all their own.

There are six types of flower in the picture — large and small roses, fuchsia, iris, anemone and gypsophila — together with green lace leaves. All the flowers (except the gypsophila), and the lace leaves, are made with the same, basic wire stem technique.

Materials required
For each type of flower
Large rose: 60cm (24in) of 5cm (2in)-wide lace edging
Small rose: 20cm (8in) of 2.5cm (1in)-wide lace edging
Anemone: 15cm (6in) of 5cm (2in)-wide lace edging
Fuchsia: 25cm (10in) of 3.5cm (1¼in)-wide lace edging
Iris: 20cm (8in) of 5cm (2in)-wide lace edging
Gypsophila: single motifs cut from a strip of guipure edging
Leaf: cut shape from a length of 5cm (2in)-wide lace beading

Fig 1 *Bend the end of the stem wire to make a small loop and thread binding wire through. Twist the short end down the stem, then wire a tiny piece of cotton wool over the loop for all flowers except gypsophila*

Fig 2 *Wind the lace around the loop to make a tube and secure with wire*

Fig 3 *Petal shape for anemone*

Fig 4 *Petal shape for iris. Glue binding wire down the middle of each petal*

For all flowers
Medium-weight stem wires
Florists' binding wire
Cotton wool
Stem tape (green or white)
Stamens in mixed colours
Watercolour or fabric paints (optional)
All-purpose clear adhesive

Preparation
If laces are to be coloured, do this before cutting pieces. Colour the edges only, fading colour off towards the straight edge. Leave to dry.

Make a stem for each flower by bending a small loop on one end of a stem wire and threading through a 30cm (12in) length of binding wire. Twist the short end down the stem. Wire a tiny piece of cotton wool over the loop (Fig 1).

Working the designs
Large rose Roll the end of the lace round the stem loop so that the cotton wool-covered tip is near to the bottom, straight edge of the lace. Wind in a clockwise direction to make a tube of lace on the stem. Secure the bottom of the tube by winding the binding wire round two or three times (Fig 2).

Holding the stem in one hand, gather the straight edge of the lace round the bottom of the tube and turn the stem. When you have made a complete turn, wind the wire around the bottom of the flower to secure the 'petal' and continue to gather lace around the rose shape. You can open the rose shape with your fingers while making the petals. About three full turns will make an open rose like those pictured. Bind the wire tightly under the rose head and wind the remaining wire down the stem.
Small rose Make in the same way as the large rose.

Anemone Cut five petal shapes from lace edging (Fig 3). Choose a complete lace motif for each petal if possible. Bind a few stamens around the stem loop, then add the petals one by one, slightly overlapping the edges. The cotton wool 'bud' should not show, so bind in the petals tightly. Wind the wire end down the stem as for the roses.

Fuchsia Bind a few stamens around the stem loop. Cut a 5cm (2in) length of lace and fold it round the stem to make the 'bell'. Secure with wire. Gather and bind a frill of lace around the bell, opening the frill with the fingers to make the flower's petals.

Iris Cut six petal shapes from lace edging (Fig 4). Cut six lengths of binding wire and glue one down the middle of each petal. Leave to dry.

Bind a few stamens around the stem loop. Bind three petals around the loop, spacing them equidistantly. Bind the remaining three petals in between. Bend the inner petals down

and tip up the ends (see picture). Bend the outer petals up so that the tips almost meet.

Gypsophila Bind a single stamen to the tip of a straight stem wire. Slip a guipure motif on the wire and push it right up to the stamen tip. Bind the stem with tape to hold the lace motif in position. Make three to five flowers for each spray.

Leaf Prepare a stem wire (Fig 1) without the cotton wool bud. Pleat and gather the lace to the stem, binding tightly.

Finishing

All the flowers, except the gypsophila, are finished in the same way. Hold the end of the stem tape under the flower head and, slightly stretching the tape, turn the stem until the wire binding is covered, thus making a 'calyx'. Continue to turn the stem, smoothing tape to cover the length of the stem.

Leaves are finished in the same way as flowers. Two or three leaves can be bound together to make a single spray.

To finish the gypsophila, tape together the stems of three to five flowers about 5–6cm (2–2½in) below the heads.

Sweet baskets

These sweet baskets really are sweet – they are made from crochet lace mats stiffened in a solution of sugar and water. As shown in the picture, sweet baskets can also be used for fresh flowers, the lace making a crisp yet delicate contrast to the blossoms and foliage.

Materials required

Cotton crochet doilies and mats
Strips of galloon lace for handles
White sugar
Boiling water
Moulds such as plastic, glass or pottery bowls, dishes, tumblers, etc
Rust-proof pins
Board or other suitable surface for pinning out lace
Spray varnish (optional)

Preparation

Mix two tablespoons of sugar with one tablespoon of boiling water. Stir until all the sugar is dissolved. Dip the piece of dry lace in the solution, making sure every part is soaked. Squeeze out gently. (When making larger quantities of sugar and water solution for several lace pieces keep the proportions the same.)

Working the design

Stand the selected mould on the board. Place the soaked and squeezed-out lace over the mould, pressing and stretching it over the shape. Wrap and tie string around the shape to keep the lace close against the mould. Shape the edges of the lace by pulling them gently, pinning at the points (Fig 1). When the lace is almost dry, the edges and points can be shaped again.

Making handles

Mix more sugar and water solution and soak a strip of lace in it. The handle on the basket containing flowers is made from a strip of lace 38cm *(15in)* long.

Leave the lace to dry flat on the

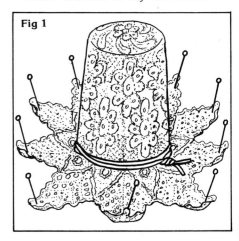

Fig 1

board, but, as it dries, shape it gently into a curve.

Stitch or glue the handle to the sides of the basket.

Finishing

If baskets are to be used for fresh flowers, replace the original mould in the basket for a water container.

Moisture will eventually make the sugar-stiffened lace a little sticky, so spray-varnish any baskets that are to be used to contain water.

Sugar-stiffened baskets can be washed if they become soiled — but of course the sugar will wash out and the lace will have to be stiffened and shaped again.

Fig 1 *Tie string around the mould to shape the lace and pin out the points*

More ideas for sugared lace

Basket handles

Basket handles may also be made from plaited lace insertion or lace beading. Thread ribbon through the holes after the lace has been stiffened and dried (Fig 1). Gathered galloon lace also makes a pretty handle. Gather the lace first before soaking it in sugar solution.

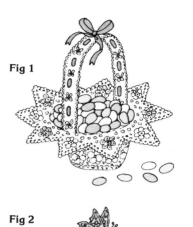

Fig 1

Cake decorations

Cotton lace motifs, dipped in sugar solution, make pretty cake decorations. Choose butterfly motifs, for instance, bending the wings as though in flight, or group flower motifs together, securing them to the cake with icing (Fig 2).

Cotton lace can be tinted with food colouring (see page 41) before sugaring.

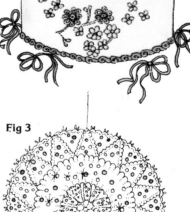

Fig 2

Christmas decorations

Small crochet lace doilies and mats make beautiful 'snowflakes' for Christmas windows. Soak them in sugar solution and dry flat. Glue sequins or glass beads to the mats, then suspend them on silver thread or invisible nylon thread (Fig 3).

Small Christmas tree trims can be made from lace edgings and insertions. Form shapes over small containers, as described for making the sweet baskets, or weave narrow laces in a basket effect over polystyrene balls (Fig 4).

Lace lampshade

A pretty lampshade can be made over an inflated balloon. Soak strips of lace beading in sugar solution and dry them over the balloon. Thread ribbon through beading. Glue or sew the strips together when they are dry to make an openwork ball lampshade (Fig 5).

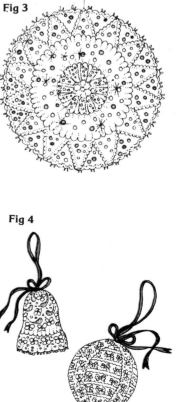

Fig 3

Fig 5

Fig 4

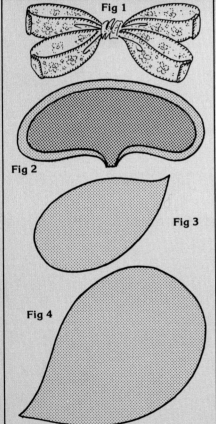

Fig 1 *Sew two pairs of loops together with the joined ends at the bow's sides*

Fig 2 *Large and small petal shapes for rose*

Fig 3 *Leaf shape for rose*

Fig 4 *Petal shape for peach lapel flower*

Lace jewellery

Lace shaped with wire is a Victorian craft and was used to make floral accessories for hats and clothes. Silk was sometimes used with the lace to provide textural contrast and colour.

Hair bow

Materials required

Finished size 12.5cm (5in) wide
66cm *(26in)* of 4cm *(1½in)*-wide lace insertion
1.50m *(1⅝yd)* fine wire
Hair comb, beads, sequins
All-purpose clear adhesive

Preparation

Cut four pieces of lace each 15cm *(6in)* long. Cut four pieces of wire each 35cm *(14in)* long.

Working the design

Stitch a wire along the long edge of a piece of lace (see Lacecraft Techniques 4). When you reach the short end of the lace, bend the wire at right angles and stitch the wire across the width of the lace. Then continue along the other long edge. Join the ends of the wired strip by overlapping the wired end and the unwired end and slipstitching together.

Form the wired lace into a circle, then flatten the circle in your hands with the join at one end to make a loop. Make three more lace loops in the same way.

Sew two pairs of wired loops together (Fig 1). Sew the loops to the comb, taking the threads over the comb and through the teeth. Stitch a small piece of lace insertion over the join to make the bow's knot. Glue on sequins and sew on beads for glitter.

White rose

Materials required

Finished size 8cm (3¼in) wide
Small piece of white patterned net
10cm *(4in)* of 12mm *(½in)*-wide white lace edging
Scrap of white cotton lace
45cm *(18in)* of 3mm *(⅛in)*-wide white satin ribbon
Fine wire
Silver thread
Silver glitter dust, silver sequin, large pearl bead
All-purpose clear adhesive
Tracing paper

Preparation

Cut a 25cm (10in) length of wire. Thread the bead on to the wire and push it to the middle. Bend the wire in half and twist together to make a stem. Glue the sequin to the top of the bead.

Trace the two petal shapes (Fig 2). Cut wire to fit three large and two small shapes, with 2.5cm (1in) stems. Cut three large and two small shapes from net with 3cm (1¼in) extra all round.

Trace the leaf shape (Fig 3). Cut wire to fit and cut shape from cotton lace, as for the petals.

Working the design

Apply the wire to the pieces of net to make the petals (see Lacecraft Techniques 4). Apply wire to the cotton lace for the leaf in the same way.

Glue the end of the lace edging round the pearl bead and when the glue is dry sew the lace round the bead to make the centre of the rose.

Bend a small petal round the rose centre and sew it in place, then snip off the wire ends. Sew a second small petal round the centre, then add the three large petals in the same way,

overlapping the edges (see picture). Fold back the edges of some of the petals for a natural look.

Glue a small piece of cotton lace behind the rose head for a calyx.

Finishing

Wrap and glue the satin ribbon round the stem, binding in the leaf as you work. Wind silver thread over the ribbon (see picture). Paint a little glue on some of the petals and sprinkle on glitter dust.

Peach lapel flower

Materials required

Finished size 11cm (4½in) wide
Small piece of coloured all-over lace
10cm (4in) of 12mm (½in)-wide coloured lace edging
30cm (12in) of 12mm (½in)-wide matching satin ribbon
Fine wire
4 pearl beads
Brooch fastening or safety pin
All-purpose clear adhesive
Tracing paper

Preparation

Trace the petal shape (Fig 4). Cut wire to fit five shapes, with 2.5cm

(1in) stems. Cut five shapes from all-over lace with 3cm (1¼in) extra all round.

Working the design

Apply the wire to the pieces of lace (see Lacecraft Techniques 4).

Gather the lace edging and sew it into a double-layer circle for the flower centre. Glue the pearl beads in the middle of the flower centre.

Sew the petals around the gathered lace circle, bending the petals (see picture).

Finishing

Sew the ribbon behind the flower centre to make a loop and two ends. Fish-tail the ribbon ends. Sew the brooch fastening or safety pin at the back of the flower.

LACECRAFT 4 TECHNIQUES

Wiring lace

Fine flexible wire of any kind can be used but covered milliners' wire produces the best results. Spray-starch cotton lace and iron before wiring.

Straight edges This technique is used for the hair bow.

1. Lay the wire along the edge of the lace.
2. Work a medium-width but close zigzag stitch over the wire.

Shaped pieces This technique is used for making flower petals, leaves, etc.

1. Draw the shape required on paper.
2. Bend the wire to the shape and twist the ends together to make a stem so that the piece can be handled easily.
3. Cut a piece of lace to the shape with 3cm (1¼in) extra all round.
4. Place the wire on the lace and, holding it in position with the fingers, work narrow zigzag stitch over the wire, excluding the wire ends. Snip the excess lace away beyond the stitching.
5. Re-set the sewing-machine to a close zigzag stitch and stitch round again to neaten the edges.

Hand-sewing wired lace The techniques described can also be worked by hand, using a close buttonhole stitch.

Flight of birds

Little birds with lacy wings and tails make a pretty mobile for a baby's room. The same design, worked with lace dyed brown, could make a robin mobile for Christmas.

Materials required

Finished size 23cm (9in) diameter
For the mobile
23cm (9in)-diameter lampshade ring with struts
Lampshade tape for binding frame
1m (1⅛yd) scallop-edged guipure trim
1m (1⅛yd) flower-motif embroidery trim
5cm (2in) square macramé lace
Strong, white button thread
All-purpose clear adhesive
For each bird
5×6cm (2×2½in) thin, white card
8cm (3¼in) of 18mm (¾in)-wide lace edging for wings
15cm (6in) of 15mm (⅝in)-wide lace insertion for tail
2 small guipure flowers
Tracing paper
Felt-tipped pen

Preparation

Trace the bird shape (Fig 1) and draw it on card, marking the points A, B and C and the V-shaped notch at the tail end. Pierce the holes at A, B and C. Cut out the shape for a template. Use the template to draw the bird's body on the thin white card and pierce holes A, B and C with a needle. You may make any number of birds for the mobile — the one in

the picture has 14.
    Cover the lampshade ring with tape, sewing the ends.

Working the design

Glue the guipure trim round the lampshade ring. Glue the flower trim round the top edge. Cut macramé lace to cover the central ring and oversew to the tape.
    Tie three lengths of strong button thread to the central ring and knot together at the top. Hang the ring ready for attaching the birds.

Making the birds

The lace wings must be exactly the same length or the birds will not hang level. Cut the lace edging into two pieces, exactly the same length.
    Thread a needle with sewing thread and tie a knot in the end. With running stitches gather the straight edge of one wing piece, then pass the needle through the hole at A and continue gathering up the second wing piece. Pass the needle through hole B and then through the knotted thread end. Draw the thread up gently and the wings will lie against the sides of the bird's body (Fig 2). Make another knot to secure the thread end and cut it. Work all the birds' wings in the same way.
    To make the tail fold the lace insertion in four and gather with small stitches (Fig 2). Push the gathered point into the V-shaped notch at the tail end of the bird's body. Stitch through the card to hold the tail secure (it should stand up a little behind the bird). Glue a guipure flower to each side of the tail where it joins the body.

Finishing

Draw in the eyes, beak and a few breast feathers with the felt-tipped pen.
    Thread a needle with a length of button thread. Knot the end. Pass the needle through hole C on the bird's back and pull the thread through until the knot lies against the bird's body. Put a dab of glue to hold the knot and cut off any excess thread ends. Sew the other end of the thread to the lampshade ring.

Balancing the birds

Vary the lengths of the suspending threads so that the birds fly at different heights.
    Sew two birds to the central ring. Tie them loosely first until the ring is level, then sew in position. Three more birds are fixed to the struts. Tie each loosely to make certain of balance, then sew each one in turn. The remaining nine birds are spaced equidistantly round the outer ring (see picture).

Fig 1 *Trace the bird shape on card and cut out for a template*

Fig 2 *Attach lace wings through holes at points A and B. Fit the gathered lace tail into the V-shaped notch*

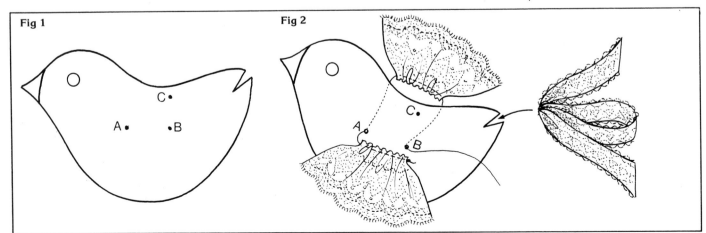

Fig 1   Fig 2

Lace of many colours

Lace is traditionally made in white, cream, ecru or black and coloured laces are rarely available. However, there are occasions when the use of coloured lace may produce a more subtle or sophisticated effect.

Home furnishings, for instance, often require a coloured lace trim when the fresh prettiness of white or cream lace may not suit the furnishing style. Bed linen and towels can come into this category, together with curtains and window blinds.

Window blind

The window blind in the picture shows how a modern colour styling can be achieved by the use of lace dyed to tone with the fabric. Two pieces of heavy, macramé-type furnishing lace have been joined on the straight edges and dyed from the original ecru with a multi-purpose chemical dye in Seville Orange colour.

Dyeing lace

Chemical dyes are suitable for almost every kind of fibre, but polyester and acrylic do not dye well. Cold-water dyes are best for fine fabrics, such as silk or cotton lawn, which may not stand up to simmering. These dyes are also very colour-fast and are ideal for items that will be laundered frequently.

Multi-purpose dyes can be used for both man-made and natural fibre fabrics, but on man-made fabrics the dye may not produce the strength of colour required.

When dyeing lace fabric or trimming, choose the dye type by the fibre content of the lace. Unless the lace is all cotton, be prepared for some of the brighter shades to weaken in colour.

There may be some shrinkage when dyeing cotton or cotton-mix laces. Allow for this, and do not cut the fabric on which the lace is to be mounted or applied before measuring the dyed, dried lace.

Natural dyes

Dyes made from natural matter – plants, flowers, vegetables, seeds, skins, fruits, seaweeds, molluscs and lichens, etc – can be made fast with the addition of mordants (colour-fixing substances). Generally, naturally-dyed fabrics fade in strong light and this process is therefore unsuitable for most home furnishings. Naturally-dyed fabrics properly colour-fixed can be hand-laundered without colour-loss.

Natural dyes will only take on natural fibres, so only cotton lace can be dyed by this method.

Tea-tinting

Tea is used to tint white lace to a range of ecru colourings. (The lace on the lingerie, page 46, and on the baby gown, page 54, was dyed with tea in varying strengths.) Cotton, silk and synthetic fibre laces will all take the tea tint well and if the tinted lace is gently hand-washed in soapy water, the colour will not run. Biological washing powders and bleaches are not recommended.

Indian tea produces a darker range of colours than China tea.

Put a teabag in a pan and add two cups of cold water and a tablespoon of white vinegar. Immerse the lace and bring the liquid to a boil. After ten minutes the lace will have taken on a distinct colour but the process can be halted at any point depending on the shade required. Remember that colours look darker when wet.

For really dark shades, use two teabags to the same amount of water and vinegar.

Food colourings

Tinting lace with food colouring is almost a craft in its own right and provides considerable scope for experimentation. This technique should be used only when the lace is not to be laundered afterwards, such as for fancy dress costume trim, character dolls' clothes, collage, flower-making, cake decoration, etc.

Spread the lace wrong side up on white blotting paper and brush on the colour with a paint brush. Colours can be mixed and diluted with water. For all-over colour, pour the food colouring into a dish, dilute as required and immerse the lace.

Fabric paints

These are available as ready-to-use paint, as powder paint and in a spray. Follow the manufacturer's instructions for using fabric paints, particularly when permanent colour is required.

Spray fabric paints are effective when used to obtain shaded patterns on all-over lace.

Car paint sprays

Surprisingly, these paints do not stiffen lace when used for colouring. The metallic finishes are attractive used on lace, particularly for Christmas ornaments and decorations. Follow the manufacturer's instructions for using car paint sprays.

Tie-dyeing

Tie-dyed lace looks very striking and unusual, often prettier than when dyed a solid colour.

Form the lace into hanks, twist it into ropes or knot it, and tie with cotton thread. The exposed areas will dye a darker colour.

Coloured laces, from left to right:
Macramé lace coloured with Canary Yellow multi-purpose dye.
The same Canary Yellow dyed macramé lace quick-dipped in Black multi-purpose dye.
Leavers lace treated with cochineal food colouring, then dipped in Brown multi-purpose dye.
Raschel lace dyed in Indian tea.
Leavers lace coloured with Primrose cold-water dye.
Leavers lace coloured with Seville Orange multi-purpose dye.
Leavers lace coloured with Primrose cold-water dye, then quick-dipped in Black multi-purpose dye.
Leavers lace treated with cochineal food colouring, then quick-dipped in Black multi-purpose dye.
Cluny lace coloured with Seville Orange multi-purpose dye, then again with Rust multi-purpose dye.
Cluny lace coloured with Seville Orange multi-purpose dye, lightly bleached, then quick-dipped in Black multi-purpose dye.

Lace collage

Making pictures from scraps of lace is a comparatively new craft, made possible by the wide variety of modern lace patterns and types that are available. The collage pictured uses the crisp contrast of white lace and ribbon against a plain-coloured background to produce a formal – yet pretty – interpretation of a decorative, Victorian town house.

You can work the design from the graph pattern of the Victorian house (Fig 1). However, your own house may also make an attractive lace collage. Take a photograph and from this, make a simplified drawing of the outline. Draw in the windows and door – again very simply – then add any decorative features that you think could be interpreted into lace or ribbon. From this point, your creativity comes into play. Visit a trimmings counter, taking your sketch with you, and look through the material available, considering whether a trim can be cut into separate motifs, or be used in massed rows, to achieve the required effects.

Victorian house

Materials required
Finished size 43 × 36cm (17 × 14½in)
50 × 43cm *(20 × 17in)* satin or other fabric for backing
43 × 36cm *(17 × 14¼in)* card or board
Assorted scraps of guipure, lace edging, strips of lace motifs, broderie anglaise edging, ricrac braid, ribbon, etc
All-purpose clear adhesive and applicator stick
Squared pattern paper, 1sq = 5cm *(2in)*

Preparation
Spread the fabric wrong side up. Centre the piece of card on the fabric. Fold the fabric on to the card and glue it down, smoothing the fabric as you work. Leave to dry.

Draw the pattern (Fig 1) up to full size on squared pattern paper. Cut out the windows and door. Cut out the shape of the house.

Position the cut-out shape on the right side of the mounted fabric, the bottom of the pattern 4cm *(1½in)* from the lower edge of the mount. Hold the pattern in place with a few

Fig 1

Fig 1 *Graph pattern for the Victorian House, 1sq = 5cm (2in)*

pins stabbed into the card. Draw around the outline of the house, and the windows and door, with light pencil lines.

Working the design
Begin by glueing the roof tiles in place. A piece of guipure all-over lace was used for the collage in the picture but you could use scalloped lace edging, mounted in overlapping rows. Use only a very small amount of glue, applying it with the tip of the applicator stick. Hold the glued lace

in position with a few pins until the glue has dried.

Add the roof ridge next using a strip of ribbon, then outline the gables with the same ribbon. Pin these pieces in place while you outline the rest of the house, overlapping pieces where appropriate.

Now you can begin to add the details of the house. Let your imagination run freely, allowing the materials to inspire you to create decorative effects.

Coloured lace collage

A delightful effect is achieved by colouring lace pieces with watercolour or fabric paints for collage work. If you feel confident about your ability to pre-plan colour effects, tint the lace before assembling the collage. Otherwise, in most instances, it is acceptable to colour the lace after it has been glued down. This may, however, present some difficulties when pieces overlap.

To colour lace, work on a piece of blotting paper pinned to a surface such as a cork board or a sheet of expanded polystyrene. Use tweezers to hold pieces while they are being coloured. Dilute colours to pale tints, starting with a pale tone and building up two or three applications to obtain the required colour. Thick paint can clog the delicate strands of lace and a strong colour is difficult to remove once the paint has soaked into the lace. Use as little paint as possible on the brush.

If mistakes in colour tones occur, leave the tinted lace in a saucer of warm water for a while to allow the colour to wash out.

Pin lace pieces to the blotting paper to dry thoroughly before using them.

Cat in the window

Materials required
Finished size 24×18cm (9½ × 7¼in)
29×24cm *(11½ × 9½in)* finely woven cream fabric
24×18cm *(9½ × 7¼in)* backing board
Striped (or other) fabric for wall
Swiss embroidered fabric for foreground, dyed to colour required
Small piece of black net for window
Embroidered nylon edging for pelmet
Guipure edging for curtains
Scraps of black guipure lace for cat
Narrow braid and guipure edging for window frame and surround
Guipure and lace motifs cut from trims for flowers, leaves, buds, etc
Guipure motifs cut from trims for flower pots and bowls

Watercolour or fabric paints
Soft paint brush
All-purpose clear adhesive and applicator stick
White and blue embroidery threads

Preparation
Measure and mark the centre of the cream fabric to find the centre of the picture. Lightly pencil the window shape around the centre point. Glue the black net over the window, glueing only on the edges of the net. Glue the striped fabric next, for the surrounding wall, then the Swiss embroidered fabric on top, for the foreground.

If you are pre-tinting the lace pieces, do this now and leave pieces to dry completely.

Working the design
Collage pictures are worked from the background to the foreground, overlapping pieces as required. Assemble the picture with pins first to make sure that you have all the pieces you need for your required effect.

The picture is assembled in this order: 1. Window frame (narrow braid and guipure edging) 2. Curtains (six pieces of guipure edging for each curtain) 3. Window surround (guipure edging) 4. Pelmet (embroidered nylon edging) 5. Cat's body (black guipure lace) 6. Cat's head (embroider the eyes and whiskers on the guipure before applying) and cat's ears 7. Flowers overlapping the cat's body (guipure and lace motifs)

8. Flower pots and bowls (guipure motifs) 9. Remaining flowers and leaves.

Glue the pieces to the background with the applicator stick, using as little glue as possible. If you are tinting the lace after assembly, make sure the glue is completely dry first.

Finishing and framing

When the collage is dry, stretch the picture over the backing board, glueing down the fabric on the back. Frame as required.

While glass protects collages from dust, it can flatten the surface of lace. If glass is to be used, ask the framer to set the picture back in the frame so that there is space between glass and picture.

Basket of flowers

Materials required

Finished size 30 × 40cm (12 × 16in)

35 × 45cm *(14 × 18in)* dark blue-green fabric for background

Backing board cut to an oval shape 30 × 40cm *(12 × 16in)*

15cm *(6in)* of 7.5cm *(3in)*-wide lace edging for basket

Guipure and lace motifs cut from trims for flowers and leaves

Watercolour or fabric paints

Soft paint brush

All-purpose clear adhesive and applicator stick

Embroidery threads

Small beads (optional)

Preparation

Cut the background fabric roughly to the same shape as the oval backing board and 3cm *(1¼in)* larger all round. Snip into the fabric edges, fold over to the back of the board

and glue down. Pin if necessary to hold securely and leave to dry.

If you are pre-tinting the lace pieces, do this now and leave pieces to dry completely.

Working the design

The lace basket is positioned first. Cut the lace edging into pieces, angling the ends to form the shape of the basket (see picture). Glue in place with the applicator stick.

Pin all the flowers and leaves to achieve the desired effect, then begin glueing down the motifs, working from the outside edge of the design towards the bottom centre and overlapping pieces as required.

Some of the flowers in the picture have had stamens added with embroidered French knots. If you prefer, glue on tiny beads.

If you are tinting the lace after assembly, make sure the glue is completely dry first.

Sewing with Lace

Sewing with lace is almost an art in itself. The techniques involved in applying edgings, inserting lace, gathering edgings and working with motifs are all important to master if the finished work is to have an exquisite hand-made look.

Peaches and cream lingerie

A touch of lace on hand-made clothes gives them a special look of elegance and charm. Choose superb fabrics – like the shimmering polyester satin used for the lingerie pictured – and select the perfect lace to complement the colour and texture of the fabric. The wide lace insertion used with the peach satin was tinted a creamy, tan colour with tea (see page 41 for technique).

Materials required
To fit sizes 12-14. (To adapt the patterns, see page 49)
3m (3¼yd) of 120cm (48in)-wide polyester satin fabric
2m (2¼yd) of 8cm (3¼in)-wide double wide lace insertion **or** 4m (4½yd) of 5cm (2in)-wide galloon lace
Waist elastic (to fit waist, twice)
Squared pattern paper, 1sq=5cm (2in)

Preparation
Draw the patterns for the camisole and French knickers (Fig 1 overleaf) up to full size on squared pattern paper. Mark all annotation and the fabric direction arrows on the pattern pieces.

Draw a paper pattern for the waist slip following the diagram (Fig 1 below). Mark all annotation and the fabric direction arrow.

A seam allowance of 15mm (⅝in) has been included on the patterns. Cut out the pattern pieces.

Preparing the fabric
The lingerie is cut on the bias to give a perfect fit. Lay the fabric flat and make sure that the ends are cut straight. Take the top right-hand corner and fold it over until the cut edge lies on the selvedge (Fig 2). Mark the fold with long basting stitches.

Open up the fabric and fold the bottom left-hand corner up to the selvedge. Mark the fold with basting stitches. These lines of basting stitches will help you to lay your pattern pieces correctly on the true bias.

From the satin fabric cut two knickers Fronts and two Backs. Cut two camisole pieces and one camisole Front Panel piece. Using the waist slip pattern, cut two pieces, a Front and Back. Mark but do not cut the slit on the Front piece. The waist slip pattern is for a 62cm (24½in) length; adapt the length as required. Cut strips of satin fabric for rouleau straps or use 6mm (¼in)-wide ribbon.

French seams (see Fine Sewing Techniques overleaf) are used throughout the making-up instructions.

Making the waist slip
Join the side seams. Turn a 12mm (½in) casing hem on the waist edge and zigzag-stitch the hem, leaving a gap in the seam for inserting elastic.

Apply the wide lace insertion (see Lacecraft Techniques 5, page 49), stitching lace around the hem to the marked slit, then to the sides and top of the slit (Fig 3).

Insert the waist elastic and close the seam.

Making the camisole
Stitch the Centre Back seam A-B (see Fig 1 overleaf). Insert the Front Panel C-D, C-D.

Apply the wide lace insertion (see Lacecraft Techniques 5, page 49), basting the lace around the top edge of the camisole. Make small V-shaped tucks at the sides and over the Front Panel so that the lace lies flat on the fabric. Hand-sew the tucks and complete the appliqué.

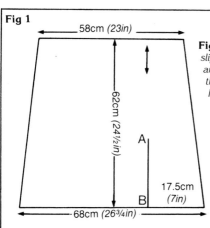

Fig 1

58cm (23in)

62cm (24½in)

17.5cm (7in)

A

B

68cm (26¾in)

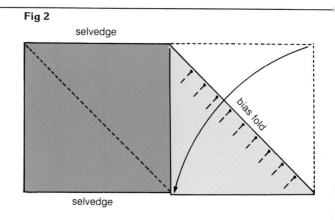

Fig 2

selvedge

bias fold

selvedge

Fig 1 *Diagram pattern for the waist slip Front and Back. The double arrow shows bias of fabric. Mark the slit (A-B) 25cm (10in) long on Front piece only*

Fig 2 *Finding the true bias on fabric*

Fig 3 *Wide lace insertion is applied to the waist slip hem, then to the sides and top of the slit*

Fig 3

Fine sewing techniques

French seams

These neat seams are best used on garments made of fine fabrics.
1. With wrong sides of fabric facing, baste and then machine-stitch 9mm (3⁄8in) from the edge.
2. Trim the seam allowance to 3mm (1⁄8in) (Fig 1).
3. With right sides of fabric together, press along the seam line, then baste along the seam line.
4. Hold the seam to the light so that the cut edges can be seen and baste along the line of the cut edges.
5. Stitch just outside the second, basted line (Fig 2). Remove basting stitches.

Shell-stitched hem

This pretty finish can be used on light and medium-weight fabrics.
1. Working from the wrong side of fabric, and starting with a backstitch,
roll the hem towards you.
2. Make two stitches over the rolled hem, bringing the needle out towards you just below the edge of the hem.
3. Take the needle through the rolled hem and bring it out under the hem about 6mm (1⁄4in) away, ready to make the next double stitch (Fig 3).

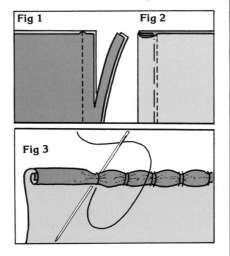

Position a second piece of lace 6mm (1⁄4in) below the top band on the Front Panel. Match the shaped heading of the lace and appliqué by hand, using whip stitches (see Lacecraft Techniques 1, page 8). Work shell stitching along the waist edge of the camisole (see Fine Sewing Techniques).

Making the French knickers

Join one Front to one Back on the crotch seam a-B, then join the other Front to the other Back on the crotch seam.

Join the two halves of knickers in one continuous seam from waist A through the crotch to A.

The side seams of the knickers are open to the waist and trimmed with lace. Apply wide lace insertion to both edges of the side seams (see Lacecraft Techniques 5).

Fig 1 *Graph pattern for the camisole and knickers, 1sq = 5cm (2in)*

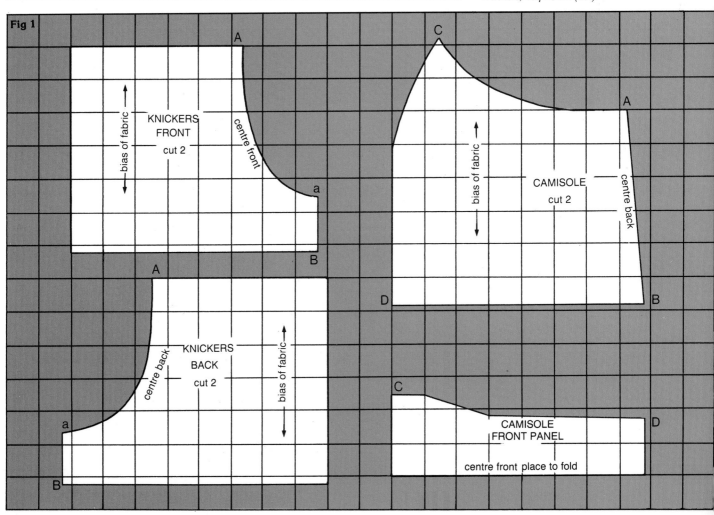

Finish the leg hems with shell stitching as for the camisole.

Turn a 12mm (½in) hem casing on the waist edge and insert elastic. Make a fabric or ribbon bow and sew to the centre waist.

Adapting the patterns

Camisole (Fig 1) To adapt to size 16, draw a new line 2.5cm (1in) outside line A-B for Centre Back seam. To adapt to size 10, draw a new line 2.5cm (1in) inside line A-B.

French knickers (Fig 1) To adapt to size 16, draw a new line 12mm (½in) outside line A-a on both Front and Back patterns. To adapt to size 10, draw a new line 12mm (½in) inside line A-a on both Front and Back patterns.

Waist slip (page 46, Fig 1) To adapt to size 16, draw the side seam line 12mm (½in) away on both sides. To adapt to size 10, draw new lines 12mm (½in) inside the side seam lines.

LACECRAFT TECHNIQUES 5

Applying wide lace insertion

Wide lace insertion is used to trim the edges of soft fabrics decoratively. The lace is used to trim the Peaches and Cream Lingerie set, but it can also be used on the sleeves and hems of nightdresses and negligés, and is sometimes featured on the hems of bridal dresses.

Double wide lace insertion has two decorative edges and a wavy line of 'eyelet' holes down the centre. When the lace is cut along these holes, the wavy edge becomes the heading and is stitched to the fabric.

1. Pin and baste the lace along the raw edge of fabric on the right side so that the lace edge projects about 2.5cm (1in) beyond the fabric edge.
2. Set the machine to a short zigzag.
3. Working from the right side, stitch the lace to the fabric along the wavy heading (Fig 1). Press the work.
4. On the wrong side, carefully trim away the fabric under the lace. Cut almost up to the stitches but take care not to snip into them (Fig 2).

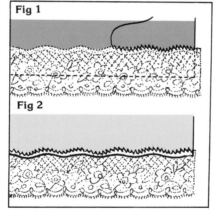

Fig 1

Fig 2

Making corners with wide lace insertion

The waist slip on page 46 has a slit at the hem and the lace has been applied to the edges of the slit meeting the hem trim in a 'mitre'.

1. To make the 'mitred' corner, stitch the horizontal hem strip of lace first, stitching to a point that will be the inner corner of the 'mitre' (Fig 3).
2. Overlay the vertical strip of lace and stitch to the same corner point. Trim the fabric away under the lace.
3. Zigzag-stitch from the corner point to the edge of the lace (Fig 4). Cut away the excess lace underneath.

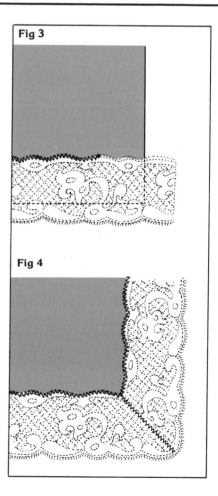

Fig 3

Fig 4

Pretty things

Here is a collection of lace-trimmed accessories to make for your bedroom, or to give away as gifts.

Soft tray

Materials required

Finished size 12.5cm (5in) square, 5cm (2in) deep
30cm (12in) of 120cm (48in)-wide polycotton fabric
23cm (9in) square pelmet-weight interfacing
1m (1⅛yd) of 18mm (¾in)-wide broderie beading
1m (1⅛yd) satin ribbon to fit beading
1.50m (1⅝yd) broderie edging (decorative edge about 18mm (¾in) deep)
Pattern paper

Preparation

Draw the round-cornered pattern (Fig 1) and cut this shape from fabric twice, with 15mm (⅝in) all round for seam allowance. Cut away the shaded areas from the pattern at the corners and use the pattern to cut the tray stiffening from interfacing (Fig 2).

Working the design

Join the short ends of the broderie edging with a straight seam and baste round one piece of fabric, right sides facing and matching straight edges. Lay the second fabric piece on top, right side down. Baste then stitch all round on three sides on the seam line. Remove basting, turn to right

side, press and insert the interfacing. Close the open side with stitching.

On one side of the stiffened fabric piece, mark the bottom of the tray, 12.5cm (5in) square (Fig 2). Machine-stitch the square shape with two rows of straight stitching.

Turn the piece over and baste the broderie beading all round the piece, mitring the corners (see page 9 for technique), and positioning it about 15mm (⅝in) below the edge of the tray. Machine-stitch on both edges.

Finishing

Thread the ribbon through, pulling the corners in and forming a tray. Tie ribbon ends in a bow on one side.

Handkerchief or tissue purse

Materials required

Finished size (without ruffle) 16 × 20cm (6½ × 8in)
20 × 42cm (8 × 16½in) polyester satin fabric
20 × 42cm (8 × 16½in) lining fabric
20 × 42cm (8 × 16½in) thin polyester wadding
20 × 42cm (8 × 16½in) heavy interfacing
2m (2¼yd) of 6.5cm (2½in)-wide galloon lace
20cm (8in) of 4.5cm (1¾in)-wide galloon beading
30cm (12in) satin ribbon to fit beading

Preparation

Mark two lines across the interfacing, one 14cm (5½in) and the other 29cm (11½in) from one short end. Mark the middle of the other short end, then round off the corners of that end.

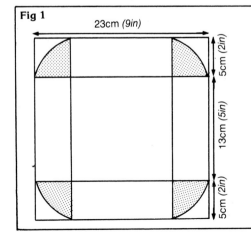

Fig 1 *Pattern for the soft tray. Draw a 23cm (9in) square and round off the 5cm (2in) corners. Cut two pieces from fabric*

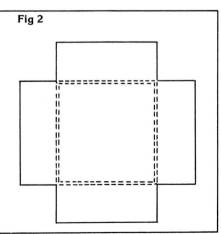

Fig 2 *Adapt the pattern for the interfacing, by cutting away the corners shaded in Fig 1. The bottom of the tray is marked with two rows of straight stitching*

Working the design

Machine-stitch twice on the ruled lines with about 1.5mm (*¹⁄₁₆ in*) between each row of stitching.

Pin the wadding to one side of the interfacing and the lining to the other, trimming to shape on the rounded corners. Baste and then stitch the edges with an open, narrow zigzag stitch.

Pin the straight edge of the satin fabric to the short straight edge of the wadding-covered side, right side up. Pin all round, then trim the rounded corners to shape. Baste all round the edges, remove the pins, then stitch all round with close zigzag stitch at its widest setting.

Pin the beading across the flap, cut off the ends and machine-stitch in place. Thread ribbon through, cut away the excess ribbon and sew the ends to the beading.

Machine-gather the galloon lace (see Lacecraft Techniques 1, page 8). Draw up the threads to fit the gathered lace round the bag on the right side, except the short straight edge. Topstitch the galloon, working about 9mm (*³⁄₈in*) from the edge (see picture).

Fold the bag in three. Fold back the galloon ruffle so that it is not caught in the stitching and oversew the bag's side seams.

Finishing

Make a small bow from the remaining ribbon and sew to the centre of the flap of the bag.

Soft-touch hanger

A well-padded hanger not only looks pretty but it is also kind to clothes made of delicate fabrics.

Materials required

Wooden hanger
50cm (*20in*) of 120cm (*48in*)-wide polyester wadding
45 × 25cm (*18 × 10in*) polyester satin fabric
1.85m (*2yd*) of 7.5cm (*3in*)-wide galloon lace
60cm (*24in*) of 2.5cm (*1in*)-wide double face satin ribbon
45cm (*18in*) of 1.5mm (*¹⁄₁₆ in*)-wide double face satin ribbon

Preparation

Cut strips of wadding about 5cm (*2in*) wide and thickly bind the wooden hanger until it has a circumference of about 17cm (*7in*). Sew ends of wadding to secure them.

Cut a piece of wadding to the overall length of the padded hanger by the circumference. Make a hole in the centre, slip it over the hook and sew the edges together on the underside of the hanger.

Working the design

Cut a piece of ribbon the length of the hook plus 2.5cm (*1in*). Fold the ribbon along the length and stitch the long edges and one short end together. Turn right side out and slip over the hook, catching the bottom end of the tube to the wadding.

Measure the padded hanger and cut a piece of fabric to the overall length plus 18mm (*¾in*) by the circumference plus 18mm (*¾in*).

Round off the corners. Zigzag-stitch the edges to neaten. Measure and find the middle of the piece. Cut a hole and buttonhole stitch the edges to neaten.

Join the ends of the galloon lace, then machine-gather one edge, stitching about 12mm (*½in*) from the edge (see Lacecraft Techniques 1, page 8). Pull up the threads to fit the ruffle round the satin piece.

Baste the ruffle to the right side of the fabric, positioning the ruffle so that the gathered edge is about 12mm (*½in*) from the neatened edge. Stitch the ruffle with a small zigzag stitch, working over the same stitching line as the gathers.

Slip the cover on the padded hanger. Fold back the lace ruffle and oversew the fabric edges together round the hanger.

Finishing

Tie a ribbon bow round the hook. Thread a large-eyed needle with the narrow ribbon and take a single stitch through the hanger from the top side and then back, tying ends in a bow. Make five bows as pictured.

Brooch cushion

This is made with a small basket about 12.5cm (*5in*) in diameter. Line the basket with a piece of polyester satin fabric, fill with wadding and then sew a satin-backed lace mat to the edges of the basket to cover the wadding.

Sew narrow ribbon round the basket, tying ends in a bow.

Weddings and lace

Lace is as much part of weddings as flowers and ribbons, bringing old-world charm and prettiness to everything from bridal clothes and bouquets to the church decoration itself. Here are some ideas for using lace at weddings.

Lace fan

Some brides prefer elegant accessories to flowers for themselves and their attendants. Plastic fan frames can be purchased and covered with all-over lace. Spread the fan on paper and trace the shape (Fig 1). Cut out the paper shape for a pattern and cut out from all-over lace. Sew the lace to the frame if there are holes for this purpose or spread clear glue on the struts and press the lace to the frame. Finish the curved edge with a gathered lace ruffle or cut-out lace motifs. Tie ribbon in a bow on the handle, leaving streamers.

Lace-trimmed parasol

A simple, yet pretty, parasol can be made with a long-handled pastel-coloured umbrella (Fig 2). Sew a double ruffle of 7.5cm (3in)-wide lace edging round the umbrella, right on the edge, then add a small gathered ruffle round the ferrule. Tie a ribbon bow to the handle.

Flower ball

Choose a white polystyrene ball about 10cm (4in) diameter. Bend the end of a 30cm (12in) rose stem wire into a loop. Push the wire through the ball so that the loop lies against the bottom of the ball. Bend a loop on the other end of the wire. Make wired lace rosettes with 20cm (8in) lengths of 12mm (½in)-wide lace edging, twisting florists' binding wire round the bottom of the rosette (Fig 3), then push the wire stems into the ball. Cover the ball with lace rosettes and push artificial flowers between the rosettes for colour. Tie ribbon bows to the bottom loop, leaving streamers, and tie a ribbon handle to the top loop.

Posy frill

Sew a 45cm (18in) length of 10cm (4in)-wide lace edging into a circle. Gather the lace into a frill, then spray-starch and iron. Push the finished lace frill on to bunched flower stems, bind stems and tie a ribbon bow underneath (Fig 4).

Brides' tiaras and circlets

Beautiful head-dresses can be made of stiffened circles of wide cotton lace edging (Fig 5). The technique for stiffening lace is on page 34.

Sashes

Use wide lace insertion for making sashes (think of it as 'lace ribbon'). Sew the lace to the matt side of single face satin ribbon. The two fabrics together can be tied into a crisp bow (Fig 6).

Something blue . . .

Make a bride's **Petticoat Knot** with two or three lace rosettes gathered and stitched to a length of 6mm (¼in)-wide blue satin ribbon (Fig 7). Pin the ribbon end to the waistband.

A **stocking garter** can be made with a 71cm (28in) length of wide galloon beading lace and blue ribbon. Machine-stitch the lace to a 38cm (15in) length of 12mm (½in)-wide elastic, overlapping the ends. Thread ribbon through the beading and tie the ends in a bow (Fig 8).

For a **simple gift**, thread a darning needle with a 1.5mm (1/16in)-wide blue ribbon and work two rows of running stitches round the edges of a fine cambric handkerchief, tying the ends in a bow at a corner. Edge the handkerchief with 12mm (½in)-wide lace, mitring the corners (Fig 9).

Lace cups

Cover plastic cups with cones of all-over lace and hang them with ribbon loops from pew ends for fresh flowers (Fig 10).

Make confetti cups (Fig 11) for guests with 20cm (8in) lengths of 10cm (4in)-wide lace edging. Gather the edge and twist wire round to make the cup shape and to secure it to a stem wire. Cover the stem with ribbon and tie a ribbon bow under the cup. Fill the cups with confetti or rice and close the open cup with a pastel-coloured paper clip.

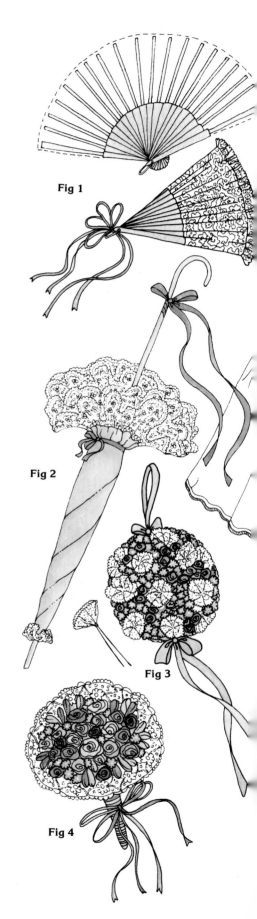

Fig 1

Fig 2

Fig 3

Fig 4

Fig 5

Fig 7

Fig 9

Fig 8

Fig 6

Fig 10

Fig 11

Heirloom baby gown

This exquisite baby gown is basically a simple design but by using a fine fabric — silk crepe de chine — together with old and new lace, an 'antique' look has been achieved. To make a gown similar to the one pictured choose a paper pattern with short sleeves and a yoke (Fig 1).

Materials required

Trimming for the baby gown pictured

30cm *(12in)* of 120cm *(48in)*-wide white tulle

53cm *(21in)* of 7cm *(2¾in)*-wide cream scallop-edged lace (old bobbin lace was used for the gown pictured) (A)

46cm *(18in)* of 18mm *(¾in)*-wide ecru lace edging (B)

1.40m *(1½yd)* of 6cm *(2½in)*-wide cream lace insertion (C)

2.15m *(2⅜yd)* of 9mm *(⅜in)*-wide ecru lace edging (D)

1m *(1⅛yd)* of 3cm *(1¼in)*-wide coffee or ecru lace edging (F)

40cm *(16in)* of 12mm *(½in)*-wide lace beading (G)

15×23cm *(6×9in)* all-over cream lace with decorative edge

Ivory double face satin ribbon as follows: 2.15m *(2⅜yd)* of 1.5mm *(¹⁄₁₆in)*-wide (E); 45cm *(18in)* of 6mm *(¼in)*-wide (H); 4m *(4⅜yd)* of 9mm *(⅜in)*-wide (I)

Squared pattern paper, 1sq=5cm *(2in)*

Preparation

Fig 2 is the graph pattern for the over-yoke, which is made of all-over lace and trimmed with lace edging and ribbon-threaded beading.

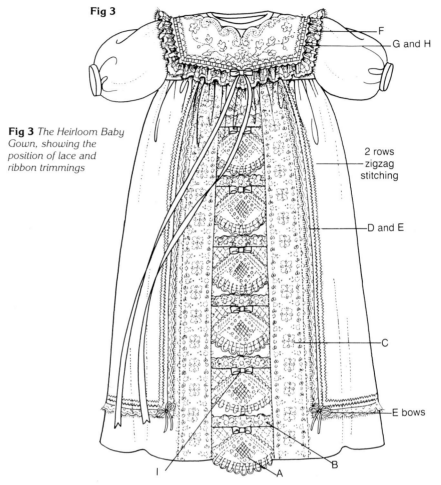

Fig 3 *The Heirloom Baby Gown, showing the position of lace and ribbon trimmings*

Draw the pattern up to full size on squared pattern paper. Cut out the pattern. Pin to the all-over cream lace so that the neck edge is on the decorative edge. Cut out one piece, adding 9mm *(⅜in)* seam allowance. Cut another piece from tulle, adding seam allowance.

From the remaining tulle cut two pieces each 60×7.5cm *(24×3in)*. Cut a piece of pattern paper to the same size.

Spray-starch and iron cotton lace. Cut scalloped lace A into seven pieces 7.5cm *(3in)* wide. Cut lace edging B into six pieces 7.5cm *(3in)* wide.

Cut lace insertion C into two pieces each 63cm *(25in)* long. Gather lace edging F (see Lacecraft Techniques 1, page 8) and leave gathering threads for the moment.

Working the design

Fig 3 shows the position and arrangement of the lace and ribbon trimmings. Arrange laces A and B in alternate rows on the pattern paper, butting straight edges. Mark where the pieces of lace lie. Pin the paper under the two layers of tulle. Now baste the laces A and B in position on the tulle.

Zigzag-stitch along the butted edges. Keep the backing paper in position to support the work. Work small zigzag stitches down both long sides of the panel to neaten.

Apply lace insertion C to both long edges. Overlap the lace about

Fig 1 *Choose a pattern with a gathered skirt on a yoke and short sleeves*

Fig 2 *Graph pattern for the over-yoke, 1sq=5cm (2in). Cut one from lace and one from tulle*

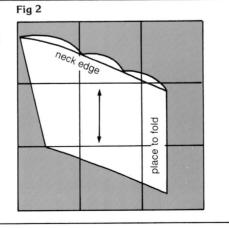

3mm (⅛in) and topstitch. The backing paper can now be torn away, working very gently at the panel edges.

Making the skirt
When cutting the skirt piece from fabric, try to arrange that both back and front are cut in one piece. Alternatively, seam two skirt pieces and arrange the seam at the back of the gown. Cut the skirt to 66cm (26in) length.

Make a 5cm (2in) machine-stitched hem on the bottom, long edge. On the two short edges turn a single narrow hem to the wrong side and zigzag-stitch to neaten.

Centre panel Lay the skirt on a flat surface, right side down, and fold the two short edges to the middle, about 7.5cm (3in) apart.

Lap the long edges of the prepared panel over the short edges of the

skirt front. Pin, baste and then topstitch.

Lace edging D and satin ribbon E are now stitched together down both sides of the panel and round the entire skirt hem, working with zigzag stitch.

To complete the panel decoration, work a row of zigzag stitches 6mm (¼in) from the ribbon E edges, using cream thread. Then work another, wider row of zigzag stitches beside the first, using ecru thread.

Neaten the bottom edge of the lace insertion C with a single hem and running stitches.

Make up the baby gown following the pattern instructions, joining yoke to gathered skirt and inserting sleeves.

Over-yoke Place the tulle and lace over-yoke pieces together, wrong sides facing. Zigzag-stitch round the bottom edge and sides, then

topstitch the neck edge (the decorative edge of the lace). Follow the lines of the lace edging as you stitch. Draw up the gathered lace F to fit round the sides and bottom edge of the yoke. Topstitch.

Stitch lace beading G over the lace edging (see picture). Thread ribbon H through the beading. Neaten the ends. Slipstitch the over-yoke to the garment yoke.

Finishing
With the remaining ribbon E make two small double bows and sew to the gown front (see Fig 3).

Make seven small stitched bows from ribbon I. Cut remaining ribbon I into two equal pieces and sew to the point of the over-yoke for streamers. Fish-tail the ends. Sew one of the small bows over the join. Sew the remaining six bows down the front of the panel.

Lace collars

Detachable lace collars are not difficult to make and they lighten the look of dresses and blouses with pretty effect. Trace-off patterns are given overleaf for making two adult-sized collars – a Peter Pan and a Puritan collar.

The same collars are given for a child, for a dress with a size 66cm (26in) chest, but the broken lines on all the patterns show where they can be adapted for other sizes.

To make the patterns smaller, fold on the broken lines and pin the fold. To enlarge the patterns, cut the patterns apart on the broken lines and pin pieces of pattern paper behind to the desired measurement.

Materials are given for making the collars from all-over lace but the collars could also be made in organdie with lace motifs applied, or from fabric with lace inserted in bands – or even from fabric made up with bands of lace insertion and beading joined edge to edge.

Materials required

Pieces of all-over lace as follows:
Adult's Peter Pan collar, 23×45cm
　(9×18in); Adult's Puritan collar,
　30×60cm (12×24in); Child's Peter
　Pan collar, 20×40cm (8×16in);
　Child's Puritan collar, 23×40cm
　(9×16in)
Pieces of lining fabric, organdie,
　organza or handkerchief lawn, to
　the same size
Soft cotton bias binding
Scraps of cotton fabric for making
　'toiles' (trial patterns in fabric)
Pattern and tracing paper

Preparation

Trace the desired pattern (Fig 1 overleaf). Mark in all annotation. Cut out the paper patterns and make any adjustment to size required.

Pin the paper patterns to folded scrap cotton fabric and draw around the shape with a soft pencil. Cut out the fabric and try the 'toile' on to see if the collar fits the neck comfortably. Make any necessary adjustments to the pattern.

Pin the collar pattern to folded all-over lace, taking note of the direction of the grain line on the pattern. Cut out 12mm (½in) away from the pattern edges.

Pin the pattern to folded lining fabric and draw around the shape with a soft pencil. Cut out 12mm (½in) away from the pattern edges.

Working the design

Pin and baste the lace piece and lining piece together, right side of lace to the fabric. Machine-stitch around the outer edges of the collar, stitching on the pencilled line on the fabric. (Do not stitch the neck edge.)

Trim the seam allowance to 6mm (¼in) and on pointed corners (such as the Puritan collar) trim away fabric at the point, almost to the stitching. Turn the collar to the right side.

Press the collar, favouring the lace side so that almost none of the fabric lining shows at the edges. Baste round the edges and then press them again. Remove the basting stitches.

From the right side of work, machine-stitch the neck edges together, stitching 3mm (⅛in) away from the seam line.

Trim the seam allowance to 6mm

(¼in) and snip into the seam allowance, almost to the stitching line so that the collar spreads and lies flat. Cut a piece of bias binding to the measurement of the neck edge plus 2.5cm (1in). Apply the bias binding to the neck edge (Fig 1), turning the ends of the bias binding to the inside. Press the binding to the wrong side of the collar.

If no fastening is to be made on the collar front, overlap the ends and work two or three bar stitches to secure (Fig 2). If a fastening is being worked, make a stitched button loop on one side of the collar and a corresponding button on the other.

Adding frilled edges

If a frilled edge is desired (see Fig 2 overleaf), gather lace edging to fit round the outer edges of the collar and baste and stitch to the lace piece. Place the lining fabric on top and finish the collar as before.

Ruffled collar

The little girl's dress in the picture has a simple ruffled lace collar, which is sewn round the neckline and can be removed easily for laundering. Any width of lace can be used. The collar in the picture is made with 7.5cm (3in)-wide galloon lace.

Preparation

Measure round the neckline of the finished garment and allow two to two and a half times this measurement in lace. Allow the same amount of 6mm (¼in)-wide velvet ribbon.

Working the design

Gather the lace 12mm (½in) from the top edge with two rows of gathering stitches (see Lacecraft Techniques 1, page 8). Adjust the gathers evenly and secure the threads so that the ruffle fits round the neckline. Turn a narrow hem on the short ends and hand-sew.

Cut ribbon to fit the ruffle plus 2.5cm (1in). Hand-hem to the ruffle, working over the gathering stitches and turning the cut ends under.

Make a small bow with streamer ends from the remaining ribbon and sew to the middle of the collar.

Sew the ruffle to the dress, with the bow at the front.

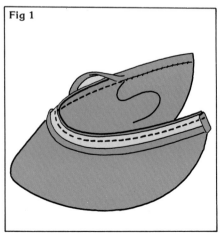

Fig 1 *Applying binding to collar neck edge*

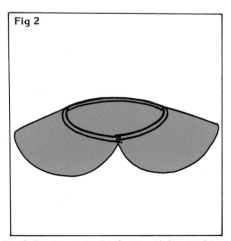

Fig 2 *Overlapping collar fronts with bar stitching*

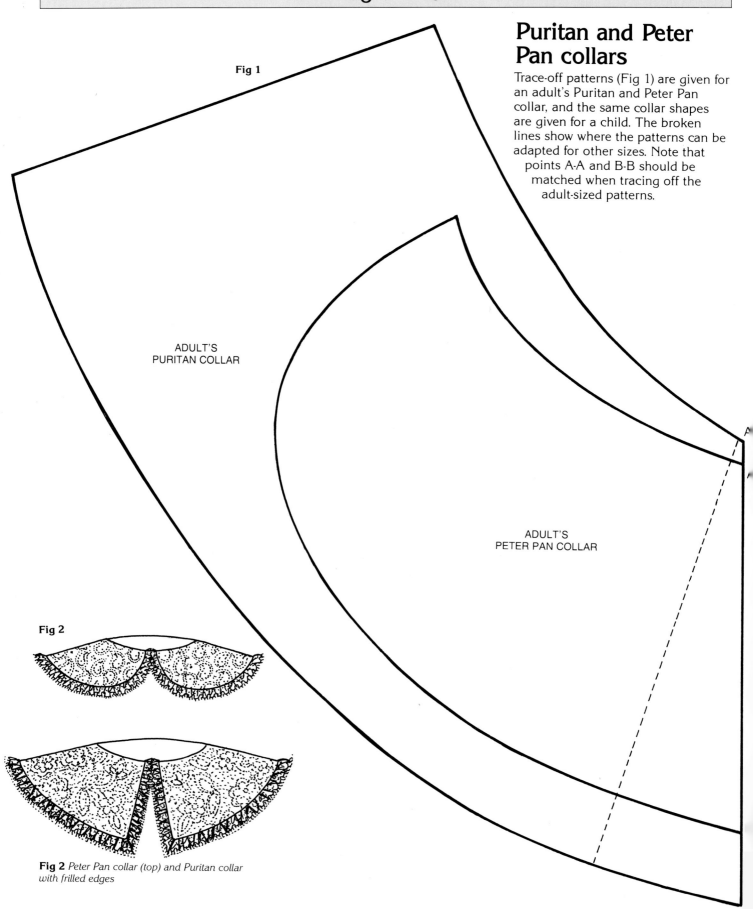

Fig 1

ADULT'S
PURITAN COLLAR

ADULT'S
PETER PAN COLLAR

Puritan and Peter Pan collars

Trace-off patterns (Fig 1) are given for an adult's Puritan and Peter Pan collar, and the same collar shapes are given for a child. The broken lines show where the patterns can be adapted for other sizes. Note that points A-A and B-B should be matched when tracing off the adult-sized patterns.

Fig 2

Fig 2 *Peter Pan collar (top) and Puritan collar with frilled edges*

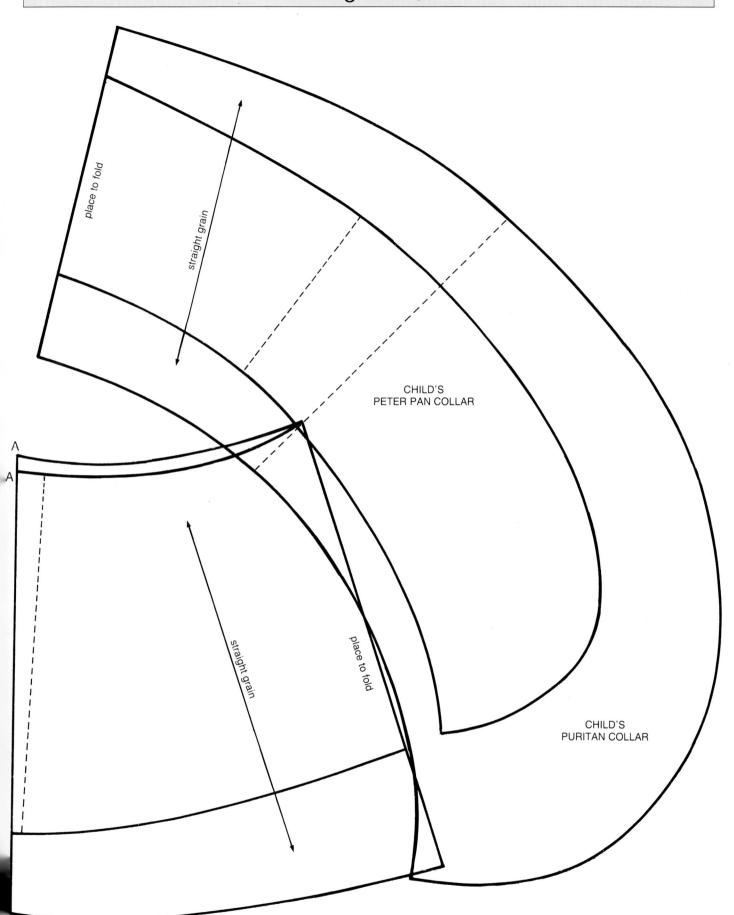

place to fold

straight grain

CHILD'S
PETER PAN COLLAR

straight grain

place to fold

CHILD'S
PURITAN COLLAR

Small and pretty

British children's clothes are treasured the world over for fine sewing and pretty, understated design. This simple undie set for a little girl could be made in an evening using a sewing-machine but, for a labour of love, make it by hand with narrow French seams and sewing fine Nottingham lace round the legs, armholes, neckline and frill with tiny hemming stitches.

Materials required

Finished size: chest 71cm (28in); waist 53cm (21in); shoulder to hem 58cm (23in)

1m *(1⅛yd)* of 120cm *(48in)*-wide fine polycotton, lawn or Swiss batiste fabric

3m *(3¼yd)* of 18mm *(¾in)*-wide cotton Nottingham lace edging

1.20m *(1⅜yd)* of 9mm *(⅜in)*-wide cotton Nottingham lace edging

1.20m *(1⅜yd)* of 1.5mm *(1/16 in)*-wide satin ribbon

30cm *(12in)* of 9mm *(⅜in)*-wide satin ribbon

Small pearl button

1m *(1⅛yd)* narrow elastic

1.10m *(1¼yd)* white cotton bias binding

Squared pattern paper, 1sq=5cm *(2in)*

Preparation

Draw the patterns for the petticoat and panties (Fig 1) up to full size on squared pattern paper. Mark in all annotation. Cut out the paper patterns. Note that 15mm *(⅝in)* seam allowances have been included on all pattern pieces.

From the fabric cut out one petticoat Front on the fold, then cut out two Backs. Cut out one panties Front and one Back, placing the pattern pieces on the fold of fabric.

From the remaining fabric cut two pieces along the length of fabric, 6cm *(2½in)* wide, for the petticoat frill. Join the two pieces on the short ends and then from this strip cut the frill 172cm *(68in)* long.

Making the petticoat

Join the two Back pieces from the hem to the black dot (see Fig 1). Neaten seam allowances and press seam open. Join Front to Back on the side seams and shoulder seams, using French seams for neatness on the inside of the garment (see Fine Sewing Techniques, page 48). Ordinary seams may be used if preferred, but finish the raw edges with oversewing or zigzag stitch.

Apply the narrow lace edging to the armholes and round the neckline (see Lacecraft Techniques 6).

On the back seam turn and press a 15mm *(⅝in)* hem to the wrong side on both edges. Neaten the raw edges

LACECRAFT 6 TECHNIQUES

Applying lace edging to fabric

This technique is used for applying a lace edging to fabric, such as round a sleeve or neckline, or for edging a fabric frill. It can also be used to apply lace edging to broderie anglaise insertion.

1. Spray-starch and iron both the cotton lace and fabric.
2. Place the lace 3mm *(⅛in)* from the raw fabric edge, right sides facing.
3. Set the sewing-machine to a zigzag satin stitch, wide enough to go into the edge of the lace and off the fabric edge (Fig 1).
4. Press the seam open.
5. On the right side, work a very fine zigzag stitch on top of the seam, to help prevent the lace edge rolling.

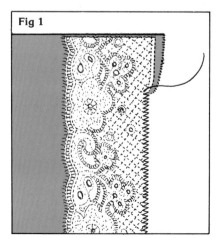

Fig 1

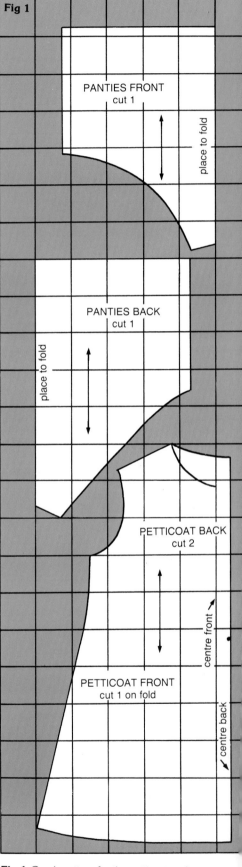

Fig 1 *Graph pattern for the petticoat and panties, 1sq = 5cm (2in)*

with oversewing or zigzag machine-stitching. Topstitch the back opening on both edges to the neckline.

Sew the button on the left side and make a hand-worked button loop on the right side to correspond.

Apply the wide lace edging to one edge of the fabric strip for the frill (see Lacecraft Techniques 6). Work a row of zigzag stitch just above the lace for decoration, or use any machine embroidery stitch. If you are working by hand, a row of Feather stitch using two strands of embroidery thread would look pretty.

Hand-pleat the frill, using basting stitches to hold the pleats, so that the frill fits the bottom edge of the petticoat. Join the ends of the frill.

Baste the frill to the petticoat, right sides facing, and machine-stitch. Trim the seam and neaten the edges with zigzag stitching. On the right side of the garment, lay the narrow ribbon just above the seam joining the frill to the petticoat and work open zigzag stitch over the ribbon. Make a tiny bow and sew to the ribbon (see picture). Make a second tiny ribbon bow for the front neck.

Making the panties

Join the crotch seam with a French seam, then sew the seam flat with hand-hemming stitches for comfort in wear. Join the side seams.

At the waist edge, turn a 6mm (¼in) hem to the wrong side and press. Then turn a slightly wider hem, press and stitch to make a casing for the elastic. Leave a gap in the seam, insert elastic to fit the waist comfortably and oversew the ends of the elastic together. Close the open seam with hand-sewing.

Apply the wide lace edging to the leg holes, following the same method as for the armholes and neckline of the petticoat.

The casing for the elastic on the legs is made with bias binding. Following the manufacturer's instructions for applying binding, make casings on the wrong side of the leg holes. Leave a gap in the stitching for inserting the elastic. Insert the elastic to fit comfortably, oversew the ends together and close the seam with hand-sewing.

Make two bows with the 9mm (⅜in)-wide ribbon and sew to the legs at the front.

Lacecraft tree trims

Soft ornaments made from fabric and lace, with sequins added for sparkle, will last for many Christmasses. They are made with a quick-sew method — enough trims for an entire tree could be made in an evening.

Materials required

Finished size approximately 10cm (4in) square

Thick polyester wadding

Pieces of fabric (satin, cotton, etc) and pieces of all-over lace:
    minimum size of pieces 10×20cm (4×8in) for all ornaments except the angels which require pieces 10×30cm (4×12in)

Scraps of trimmings, lace, guipure, ribbons, sequins, etc

Small polystyrene balls (plain white or satin thread covered)

Narrow ribbon and gold thread for hanging ornaments

All-purpose clear adhesive

Preparation

Trace the full-size shapes overleaf and cut out for patterns.

Cut pieces of fabric so that, folded in two right sides out, the patterns fit the fabric with a small surplus all round. Cut pieces of wadding to slip inside the folded fabric, sandwiching it. Pin or baste the pattern to the fabric. Pencil round the shape, then remove the pattern.

Working the design

Set the sewing-machine to 'slow'. Straight-stitch on the marked line through all thicknesses. Cut out the shape about 3mm (⅛in) from the stitched line. Work close zigzag stitch on the edges. (If no sewing-machine is available, work the first stage of stitching with running stitches and buttonhole-stitch over the edges for the second stage.)

Decorating the ornaments

Follow the picture for ways of decorating the ornaments. Other ways will occur to you as you work.
Birds These have lace motif wings, crests and tails, with sequins glued on for sparkle.

Butterflies have broderie beading bodies and hand-coloured lace motifs glued on the wings. The antennae are made by glueing wire between two pieces of 3mm (⅛in)-wide ribbon and threading the ribbon ends through the broderie beading body.
Stars The white star has a white macramé lace motif and a silver lace edging frill in the centre, and sequins on the points. The pink star, made from lace mounted over fabric, has a large organdie motif in the centre and small embroidery motifs on the points.
Bells are decorated with scraps of lace and sequins. One bell has guipure trimming stitched to the mouth; the other has lace edging stitched all the way round the shape.
Boots are decorated with lace motifs and sequins. The top edge is trimmed with a cotton lace frill and a band of lace beading threaded with gold ribbon.
Angels Nylon frilling and guipure are stitched round the curved edge. Faces are made from cream fabric, with embroidered features. Haloes and hair are made from guipure trimming. Small lace motifs complete the decoration.
Christmas balls Strips of lace are glued round some balls; others are decorated with lace flower motifs.
Baskets are made from 10cm (4in) squares of doubled fabric, top-stitched and made up in the same way as the soft tray (see page 50). They are trimmed with lace edging and the handles are made with strips of flower embroidery.

The baskets can be filled with small glass Christmas balls, sweets and candies or small gifts.

Finishing

Sew narrow ribbon in loops for hanging soft ornaments. Glue gold thread in loops for hanging Christmas balls.

More ideas for tree trims

The shapes overleaf could be cut from felt. Work decorations on the shapes before stitching together with running stitches. Stuff with cotton wool.

Shapes could also be cut from lace. Stiffen shapes in starch or sugar solution (see page 34) and hang them from silver ribbon. Alternatively, make wire shapes (see page 37) and stitch lace motifs to the wire. The lace ornaments could be decorated with pearl beads, coloured glass beads or sequins.

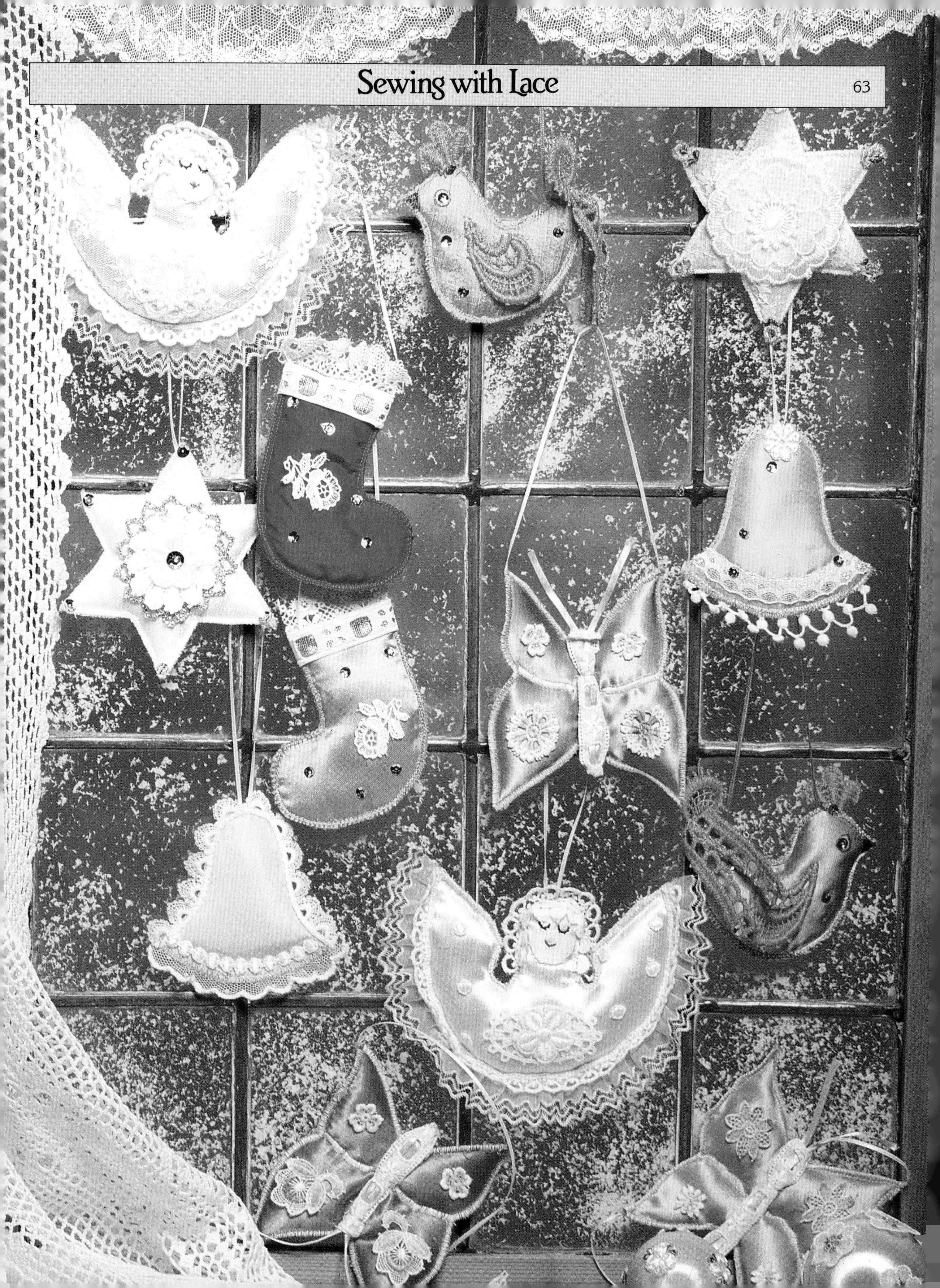

Shapes for tree trims

Trace these full-size shapes and use as patterns to make the tree trims pictured on the previous page.

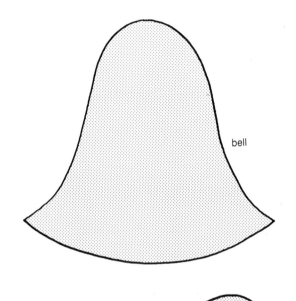

bell

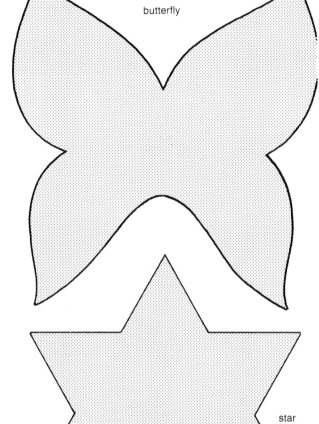

butterfly

star

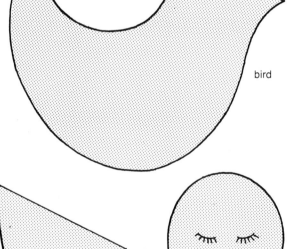

bird

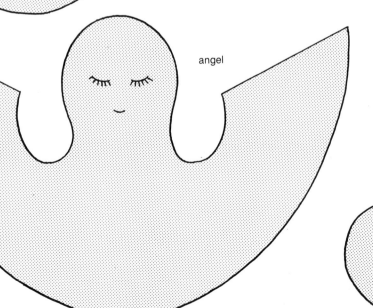

angel

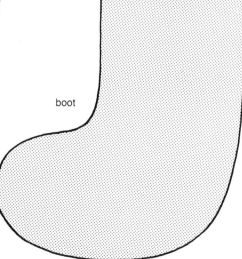

boot